MW00510835

The
INSIDER
WORKBOOK

The INSIDER

WORKBOOK

BRINGING THE KINGDOM OF GOD
INTO YOUR EVERYDAY WORLD

✳

JIM PETERSEN & MIKE SHAMY

NAVPRESS®

BRINGING TRUTH TO LIFE

OUR GUARANTEE TO YOU

We believe so strongly in the message of our books that we are making this quality guarantee to you. If for any reason you are disappointed with the content of this book, return the title page to us with your name and address and we will refund to you the list price of the book. To help us serve you better, please briefly describe why you were disappointed. Mail your refund request to: NavPress, P.O. Box 35002, Colorado Springs, CO 80935.

The Navigators is an international Christian organization. Our mission is to reach, disciple, and equip people to know Christ and to make Him known through successive generations. We envision multitudes of diverse people in the United States and every other nation who have a passionate love for Christ, live a lifestyle of sharing Christ's love, and multiply spiritual laborers among those without Christ.

NavPress is the publishing ministry of The Navigators. NavPress publications help believers learn biblical truth and apply what they learn to their lives and ministries. Our mission is to stimulate spiritual formation among our readers.

© 2003 by Mike Shamy and Jim Petersen
All rights reserved. No part of this publication may be reproduced in any form without written permission from NavPress, P.O. Box 35001, Colorado Springs, CO 80935.
www.navpress.com

NAVPRESS, BRINGING TRUTH TO LIFE, and the NAVPRESS logo are registered trademarks of NavPress. Absence of ® in connection with marks of NavPress or other parties does not indicate an absence of registration of those marks.

ISBN 1-57683-420-4

Cover design by David Carlson Design
Cover photograph by Patrick Molnar / Getty Images
Creative Team: Paul Santhouse, Karen Lee-Thorp, Nat Akin, Darla Hightower, Pat Miller

Some of the anecdotal illustrations in this book are true to life and are included with the permission of the persons involved. All other illustrations are composites of real situations, and any resemblance to people living or dead is coincidental.

Unless otherwise identified, all Scripture quotations in this publication are taken from the HOLY BIBLE: NEW INTERNATIONAL VERSION® (NIV®). Copyright © 1973, 1978, 1984 by International Bible Society. Used by permission of Zondervan Publishing House. All rights reserved. Other versions include: the *New American Standard Bible* (NASB), © The Lockman Foundation 1960, 1962, 1963, 1968, 1971, 1972, 1973, 1975, 1977; *THE MESSAGE* (MSG). Copyright © 1993, 1994, 1995, 1996, 2000, 2001, 2002. Used by permission of NavPress Publishing Group.

Printed in the United States of America

3 4 5 6 7 8 9 10 / 08 07

FOR A FREE CATALOG OF
NAVPRESS BOOKS & BIBLE STUDIES,
CALL 1-800-366-7788 (USA)
OR 1-416-499-4615 (CANADA)

CONTENTS

✳   ✳   ✳

INTRODUCTION

*　　*　　*

All Christians have inside access to a unique set of relationships. They are "insiders" to families, neighborhoods, workplaces, and social networks. You will not find their photos in church mission publications. Neither are they the subject of missionary biographies. Yet they play an indispensable role in working out God's purposes. Insiders do not need to go anywhere or join a program to have a legitimate ministry. Their ministry is right in front of them. They are key persons in moving the gospel into a family, a marketplace, or any other social context. But they are so few!

Why are there so few effective insiders? In short, there is a lack of legitimacy and encouragement to support them.

In his book *The Rise of Christianity*, Rodney Stark says, "The primary means of its [Christianity's] growth was through the united and motivated efforts of the growing number of Christian believers who invited their friends, relatives, and neighbors to share the 'good news.'"[1] Yet within three hundred years of the birth of Christianity, ministry had become the domain of the clergy.

Many of our contemporary church practices do little to encourage and enable the strategic ministry of the insider. Very few say, "Stay in there. Give your time to your unbelieving friends. We're with you."

Being authentically and meaningfully involved with unbelievers takes time and commitment. It means growing in love and compassion. For some it means developing new understandings that will redefine ministry. It requires skills to know what to do and how to do it. The insider needs support from fellow insiders as well as coaching and reinforcement from credible mentors. Above all, insiders need to keep growing in their own relationships with the Lord.

Purpose

The primary purpose of this workbook is to equip you to live fruitfully as an "insider." Specifically it will:

❖ Enrich your biblical understanding of the vital part you play as an insider in God's eternal purposes.

❖ Identify misunderstandings and obstacles that can lead to frustration and guilt in sharing your faith as an insider.

❖ Help you understand and apply the practical life patterns of an insider.

The concept of insidership is not hard to grasp. Even the biblical basis is easily taught. We have laid out these ideas in the book *The Insider* (NavPress, 2003). For most people, though, the challenge comes when they try to do what they've learned. That's why we've created this workbook—to help you put into practice what *The Insider* describes. This workbook is not primarily a Bible study, but rather a hands-on tool.

TO GET THE MOST FROM THIS WORKBOOK

Don't go it alone.

This workbook is designed to be used by a group of friends in an environment of safety and trust. Together you can strengthen and help each other as you share stories, understandings, burdens, frustrations, and encouragements. Together you can identify and apply lessons.

There are two kinds of questions in this workbook: theoretical and practical. The theoretical questions will help you digest the key concepts about living as an insider. The practical questions will help you do what you've learned. Plan to cover the theoretical questions on your own before your group meets. Read the relevant sections of *The Insider.* Then when you meet, focus your discussion on the practical questions.

Discuss the case studies, which ask you to imagine what you'd do if you were in a particular person's shoes. Discuss action you've taken in the past or could take in the future. Discuss the obstacles you face, such as busyness or fear. Encourage and support each other. It's not necessary to discuss all of the questions you've covered on your own.

Pray.

The heart is the gatekeeper of the soul. The condition of your heart will determine what you see and learn. Pray for a receptive heart.

Commit.

* *To prepare.* Each session in this workbook contains questions to consider. Record your insights and questions in the space provided. Pray for your heart to persevere and live out what you learn on your own and from others in the group.

* *To meet regularly.* Seek to be faithful in getting together. Commit to be real in the group. Be honest and open.

* *To live out what you learn as you learn.* As you trust God and implement what you are learning, new insights and questions will emerge that can shape your life as an insider. Don't wait until you have finished all the studies before you begin. Live it out as you take it in.

Seek out coaches.

The apostle Paul wrote to the insiders living in the Roman colony of Philippi: "I plan to be around a while, companion to you as your growth and joy in this life of trusting God continues" (Philippians 1:25, MSG).

Pray and look for a person who can be your companion as you grow in living as an insider. It should be a person who integrates biblical understanding in his or her life, someone who is personally living as an insider. That person can help you bridge the gap between what you are learning and how you are currently living.

YOUR UNIQUE WORLD AS AN INSIDER

FILL IN THE following chart with the names of unbelievers to whom you are an insider. These people don't need to leave anything, go anywhere, or join anything to see and hear Jesus. The invisible Christ is made visible to them through your life. Keep these people in mind as you use this workbook.

Family	Casual	Neighbors	Friends	Work Associates
-Dean + Zack + Nancy -Rory -Gary + George Amanda + Jennifer -Aunt Sally -Jeri -Sherri -Vicki -Laurie *DAD	Rob (Joanna Alberts b-friend)	Paul + Peggy	(including your kids' friends and their families) Deb Christopher Steven Kat Sam J.	(hairdresser, bank teller, store clerk)

GOD'S ETERNAL PURPOSES AND THE INSIDER

"I am my beloved's, and his desire is for me."
— SONG OF SONGS 7:10, NASB

✳   ✳   ✳

All of us need to live for something bigger than the routines of life. No matter what we achieve, we will live with a sense of futility unless what we do transcends the here and now. What's this life about? What's happening? There is only one place to go for the answer—to God himself! What is he doing in this world? A futile life is one lived by an agenda that has no connection with God's purposes.

It doesn't matter how fast we might be going, how high we think we are flying, or where we think we are headed, if we are not living according to God's purposes, ultimately our lives are futile.

> ### *The* INSIDER
>
> Along with this session, read chapter 1 of *The Insider*.
>
> What questions does this reading raise? Take your questions to your group. Make time at the end of your meeting to discuss participants' questions. If you don't have answers, keep them in mind as you read further in the book.

WHAT IS GOD ABOUT IN THIS WORLD?

EPHESIANS 1:3-10 CONTAINS vital information as to what God is doing in the world right now. The apostle Paul wrote it to a group of new believers in a corrupt society. He wanted them to understand that despite all they saw going on, God was at work and they were a vital part of God's eternal purposes.

1. Read Ephesians 1:3-10. How does Paul describe God's purpose?

Colossians 1:21-22
to present us holy &
blameless to God.

2. Jesus is central to the working out of God's eternal purposes. On many occasions Jesus stated why he came into the world. In the following passages, underline his stated purposes.

> ³Praise be to the God and Father of our Lord Jesus Christ, who has blessed us in the heavenly realms with every spiritual blessing in Christ. ⁴For he chose us in him before the creation of the world to be holy and blameless in his sight. In love ⁵he predestined us to be adopted as his sons through Jesus Christ, in accordance with his pleasure and will— ⁶to the praise of his glorious grace, which he has freely given us in the One he loves. ⁷In him we have redemption through his blood, the forgiveness of sins, in accordance with the riches of God's grace ⁸that he lavished on us with all wisdom and understanding. ⁹And he made known to us the mystery of his will according to his good pleasure, which he purposed in Christ, ¹⁰to be put into effect when the times will have reached their fulfillment—to bring all things in heaven and on earth together under one head, even Christ.
> —EPHESIANS 1:3-10

"For even the Son of Man did not come to be served, but to serve, and to give his life as a ransom for many." (Mark 10:45)

"For the Son of Man came to seek and to save what was lost." (Luke 19:10)

"God didn't go to all the trouble of sending his Son merely to point an accusing finger, telling the world how bad it was. He came to help, to put the world right again." (John 3:17, MSG) *Read NAS John 3:17*

"The thief comes only to steal and kill and destroy; I have come that they may have life, and have it to the full. I am the good shepherd. The good shepherd lays down his life for the sheep." (John 10:10-11)

GROUP EXERCISE

What are some of your frustrations and unmet expectations about sharing your faith?

What do you hope to get out of your discussions of this workbook?

What is significant to you about Jesus' stated purpose(s)?

We are/were lost/dying — we need to be rescued/saved. He didn't come to point that out, He came to save us!

3. John recorded this prayer Jesus prayed in the last days before his death and resurrection. The prayer reveals the part Jesus saw his followers playing in the outworking of God's eternal purpose. Underline the part we are to play.

> "My prayer is not that you take them out of the world but that you protect them from the evil one. They are not of the world, even as I am not of it. Sanctify them by the truth; your word is truth. As you sent me into the world, I have sent them into the world. For them I sanctify myself, that they too may be truly sanctified. *set apart (holy)*
>
> "My prayer is not for them alone. I pray also for those who will believe in me through their message, that all of them may be one, Father, just as you are in me and I am in you. May they also be in us so that the world may believe that you have sent me. I have given them the glory that you gave me, that they may be one as we are one: I in them and you in me. May they be brought to complete unity to let the world know that you sent me and have loved them even as you have loved me." (John 17:15-23)

This is an excellent reminder of Jesus ultimate priority — this is His last prayers before He died.

How would you summarize our role, as Jesus describes it?

Eph 4:2-6 — Unity
John 13:34-35 They will know by our love
Acts 2:42, 44-47 Back to our verse before
— Live holy/sanctified in unity c̄ one another

God is at work today in this world. He is bringing together a people who for all eternity will live to worship and reflect his glory. His people are in the world today for the sake of those who are not yet worshipers of God and followers of Christ.

FOR FURTHER STUDY

See how Peter describes our job description in 1 Peter 2:9-12.

read

God wants every aspect of our daily lives to be a reflection of his eternal purposes. As insiders we can participate with what God is doing in the world today, right where we are. Insiders are vital to making visible the invisible purposes of God.

Think of Wes & Penny's job - not using words to set stage for gospel - but life

OUR JOB DESCRIPTION

4. Based on what you have learned from the passages in this session, write a job description for the followers of Jesus in the world.

CASE STUDY

Jack says, "These past twenty years of my life have played out like a bad movie. As I watched them go by I kept thinking to myself, 'This wasn't the script I had in mind. It wasn't supposed to be like this.'" He pauses and adds, ". . . and I don't know what I can do to make the next twenty any different."

Professionally, Jack is highly successful. He has a good marriage and children who love him. He grew up in the church as a Christian, was part of a college campus ministry, and is now a faithful member of a local church. But he sees little to indicate that God has ever done anything through him. He was taught that God had "a wonderful plan for his life." But he hasn't seen anything happen.

What is Jack's problem?

In what ways, if any, can you identify with Jack?

Based on your study in this session, what solutions can you suggest?

Purpose:

To be a reflection of God's eternal purposes 1 Pet 2:12

Qualifications (*Who do I need to be in the process of becoming? That is, what attributes do I need to further develop?*):

Be holy 1 Pet 1:16
Unions
Compassion
Ure

Functions (*What am I supposed to do?*):

Put on the full armor of God Eph. 6:13-20

... that I might proclaim with boldness the gospel

Vital relationships (*Who do I need to help me be and do these things?*):

other believers & like mindedness Eph. 4:3
1 John 1
"Being diligent to preserve unity of the spirit"

5. What goes through your mind when you think about God inviting you to take this on as *your* job description? What immediate appeal or objections do you sense inside you?

The time & commitment
Sometimes it's discouraging &
seems hopeless. Its negativity
negativity, negativity!

> "Christianity grew through the united and motivated efforts of the growing number of Christian believers, who invited their friends, relatives, and neighbors to share the 'good news.'"[2]

Acts 2: 44·47

6. Review the past month. List the names of people with whom you have had social time: eating out or in, seeing a movie, and so on. Now put an asterisk next to the unbelievers. What does your list say about your priorities?

Shelly
Gayle
Kat*
Deb*   *not a bad balance!*
Jim
Dana

7. As you go through the next seven days, look for opportunities to say "hello" to unbelievers. Notice whether you smile. Notice whether you feel interested in them or really want to be left alone. Notice what they do. Record your observations and report them to your group the next time you meet.

GROUP EXERCISE

Take time to pray for each person in your group. Pray that you each will see how God has placed you uniquely as an insider. Ask God to overcome common obstacles to insidership, such as busyness and fear. Pray for God to work in the hearts of the unbelievers around you. As part of your prayer time, let each person finish this sentence: "Lord, one thing I need from you in this process is . . ."

→ look at list from last study

THE INSIDER AND THE KINGDOM OF GOD

* * *

Jesus came from heaven to become the ultimate insider, living among those he hoped to reach (see John 1:14). He then asked twelve people to drop all they were doing, leave their families, and "Come follow me and I will make you fishers of men" (see Matthew 4:18-22). This call to the Twelve has led to the popular notion that if a person is really serious about following Christ, then he or she should follow this example and become a pastor, priest, or missionary. Somehow this sounds more spiritual than taking him into our extended families and relational networks.

But is this how Jesus views us following him? What about all of Jesus' followers who were *not* called to leave their work and family? What did Jesus say to them?

To the man healed of demon possession he said,

"Go home to your family and tell them how much the Lord has done for you, and how he has had mercy on you." The results? "So the man went away and began to tell in the Decapolis how much Jesus had done for him. And all the people were amazed" (Mark 5:19-20).[3]

Likewise, Jesus did not invite the Samaritan woman at the well to join his traveling team. She went back to her village and told the people there about him (see John 4:28-30,39).

And in his parables, he talked endlessly about the kingdom of God and the

> *The* INSIDER
>
> Along with this session, read chapters 2 and 3 of *The Insider*.
>
> What questions does this reading raise?

24Jesus told them another parable: "The kingdom of heaven is like a man who sowed good seed in his field. 25But while everyone was sleeping, his enemy came and sowed weeds among the wheat, and went away. 26When the wheat sprouted and formed heads, then the weeds also appeared.

27"The owner's servants came to him and said, 'Sir, didn't you sow good seed in your field? Where then did the weeds come from?'

28"'An enemy did this,' he replied.

"The servants asked him, 'Do you want us to go and pull them up?'

29"'No,' he answered, 'because while you are pulling the weeds, you may root up the wheat with them. 30Let both grow together until the harvest. At that time I will tell the harvesters: First collect the weeds and tie them in bundles to be burned; then gather the wheat and bring it into my barn.'" . . .

36Then he left the crowd and went into the house. His disciples came to him and said, "Explain to us the parable of the weeds in the field."

37He answered, "The one who sowed the good seed is the Son of Man. 38The field is the world, and the good seed stands for the sons of the kingdom. The weeds are the sons of the evil one, 39and the enemy who sows them is the devil. The harvest is the end of the age, and the harvesters are angels.

40"As the weeds are pulled up and burned in the fire, so it will be at the end of the age. 41The Son of Man will send out his angels, and they will weed out of his kingdom everything that causes sin and all who do evil. 42They will throw them into the fiery furnace, where there will be weeping and gnashing of teeth. 43Then the righteous will shine like the sun in the kingdom of their Father. He who has ears, let him hear."

—MATTHEW 13:24-30,36-43

kingdom of heaven—what it is and how it grows. In this teaching we see how we can enable unbelievers to experience God's kingdom.

1. In question 7 of session 1, you were asked to spend a week paying attention to whom you greet and how you feel when you encounter people. What did you learn from that exercise? (If you didn't do it, what do you think got in your way?)

2. What ideas or pictures come to mind when you hear the phrase "the kingdom of God"?

- *Christs Reign*

3. Matthew 13:24-43 is one of Jesus' stories about how we live as citizens of the kingdom. Jesus makes clear that now is not the time to separate from the world. We are to live as citizens of the kingdom alongside the sons of the evil one. Why do you suppose God wants the wheat (us) to grow together with the weeds (unbelievers who live ungodly lives)?

4. Imagine that you could live among godly people only, completely separated from all the ungodly. How would this situation aid your spiritual growth?

How would it hinder your spiritual growth?

5. What does Jesus teach us about how we are to relate to unbelievers around us? Reflect on Matthew 5:13-16; Luke 6:27-36; Luke 14:12-14.

6. When in the past week have you had an opportunity to do one of the things Jesus names? Think particularly of a situation with an unbeliever.

Gal 6:

> [13]"You are the salt of the earth. But if the salt loses its saltiness, how can it be made salty again? It is no longer good for anything, except to be thrown out and trampled by men. [14]"You are the light of the world. A city on a hill cannot be hidden. [15]Neither do people light a lamp and put it under a bowl. Instead they put it on its stand, and it gives light to everyone in the house. [16]In the same way, let your light shine before men, that they may see your good deeds and praise your Father in heaven."
> —MATTHEW 5:13-16

> [27]"But I tell you who hear me: Love your enemies, do good to those who hate you, [28]bless those who curse you, pray for those who mistreat you. [29]If someone strikes you on one cheek, turn to him the other also. If someone takes your cloak, do not stop him from taking your tunic. [30]Give to everyone who asks you, and if anyone takes what belongs to you, do not demand it back. [31]Do to others as you would have them do to you.
> [32]"If you love those who love you, what credit is that to you? Even 'sinners' love those who love them. [33]And if you do good to those who are good to you, what credit is that to you? Even 'sinners' do that. [34]And if you lend to those from whom you expect repayment, what credit is that to you? Even 'sinners' lend to 'sinners,' expecting to be repaid in full. [35]But love your enemies, do good to them, and lend to them without expecting to get anything back. Then your reward will be great, and you will be sons of the Most High, because he is kind to the ungrateful and wicked. [36]Be merciful, just as your Father is merciful."
> —LUKE 6:27-36

Jesus told stories to help his hearers understand the kingdom of God. Like them, we too need help to see the kingdom around us. Jesus wants us to understand that we see the kingdom whenever we see people acting kingdomly; whenever, because of their love for God, they love the people in their lives.

Many people must downsize their companies; we all know people who go through divorces and end up as single moms; hundreds get cancer every day. People with needs surround us. We are so accustomed to seeing such things that we accept as normal the resentment, anger, and absorption with self that usually characterize people's responses. But we know the kingdom is among us whenever we see people, motivated by Christ's rule in their hearts, showing mercy instead of judgment, speaking the truth instead of spinning it, giving grace instead of seeking revenge, serving people instead of using them.

When we see things such as these happening, we know that God's rule is established.

—THE INSIDER, PAGE 33

People watch what Christians do and don't do, and on that basis decide whether or not they are interested in what we have. What unbeliever wants to spend his life praying, skipping meals, and giving his money away? It's not our religious activities we want people to see; it's the grace and mercy that comes from God's love that needs to show.

—THE INSIDER, PAGE 57

---

¹²Then Jesus said to his host, "When you give a luncheon or dinner, do not invite your friends, your brothers or relatives, or your rich neighbors; if you do, they may invite you back and so you will be repaid. ¹³But when you give a banquet, invite the poor, the crippled, the lame, the blind, ¹⁴and you will be blessed. Although they cannot repay you, you will be repaid at the resurrection of the righteous."

—LUKE 14:12-14

7. Imagine that you have a fifth-grade son in public school. You met your son's teacher at back-to-school night, but other than that you've had no contact with her. Your son is doing well in school, so there's been no need to confer with the teacher. It's November. How could you (with your spouse's help, if you have one) start revealing God's kingdom to your son's teacher?

JESUS LIVED AS AN INSIDER

JESUS WAS NOT a hypocrite. He lived what he taught; he illustrated his teaching by the way he lived. He had a reputation among the existing religious establishment for being good friends with some very "lost" people. Jesus, the one who was without sin and was perfect and holy, moved freely among those who were just the opposite. He did not demand people change in order to be with him socially. These social settings were vital to many people seeing and hearing his message.

8. On page 10 is a chart for listing your relationships with unbelievers. If you haven't already done so, fill out the chart.

What goes through your mind as you look at this completed chart?

> 9As Jesus went on from there, he saw a man named Matthew sitting at the tax collector's booth. "Follow me," he told him, and Matthew got up and followed him. 10While Jesus was having dinner at Matthew's house, many tax collectors and "sinners" came and ate with him and his disciples. 11When the Pharisees saw this, they asked his disciples, "Why does your teacher eat with tax collectors and 'sinners'?" 12On hearing this, Jesus said, "It is not the healthy who need a doctor, but the sick. 13But go and learn what this means: 'I desire mercy, not sacrifice.' For I have not come to call the righteous, but sinners."
> —MATTHEW 9:9-13

9. What is one small initiative you could take to strengthen a friendship with someone on that list? Perhaps you could extend yourself with an act of kindness, invite the person to share a meal, or just take time to listen to what's going on in his or her life. Look at your notes from question 5 for ideas.

INSIDERSHIP IS A PROCESS

JESUS USED FARMING images to describe how the spread of the kingdom is a process. It takes sowing, cultivating, and reaping over time (see John 4:34-38). No one puts his faith in Christ unless God has first cultivated the soil of his heart and sown seeds of God's Word into the soil. The following picture illustrates this process.

Process of Evangelism

Indifference and Antagonism

Ignorance

Indecision

CONVERSION

Living as a Disciple

GROUP EXERCISE

Think of some of the people whose names you listed on page 10. Where do you think they are in the process of journeying toward Christ? Indifferent? Ignorant? Undecided? You might want to jot notes on page 10 about where you think each person is in the process.

In the illustration, a series of obstacles stand between the unbeliever and the Cross. First he needs help to overcome his indifference or antagonism to the gospel. The soil of his hard heart needs to be broken up so that the seed can be planted and take root. Then he faces ignorance—he needs to overcome misinformation and ignorance so that he knows who Jesus really is and what Jesus really wants from him. Once he understands the gospel, he faces a decision: Will he put his life under the authority of Jesus, or will he go on trying to run his life his own way?

As you explore the life patterns of an insider, you'll see how you can help someone journey through this process.

The Insider's Role in Spreading the Gospel

* * *

Before becoming a Christian, Mary was deeply involved in student politics and the social life of her dorm. She was an insider to a unique world of relationships. Yet within two years of becoming a Christian she had become so busy in Christian activities that she was no longer available to her old friends. They felt rejected and confused by her actions. Mary is now considering full-time Christian ministry.

This might be what God wants Mary to do. We need people who are available to cross cultures with the gospel. We need people who are available to mentor and develop other believers. However, what is disturbing about Mary's story is that no one questioned the way she was relating to her unbelieving friends. No one spoke with her about the value and legitimacy of the insider. The only messages she heard were from full-time Christian workers who by their example and words communicated that the real action was somewhere else.

> ### The INSIDER
>
> Along with this session, read chapter 4 of *The Insider*. (If possible, read chapters 5 and 6 also.)
>
> What questions does this reading raise?

1. Were you able to take any initiative in a relationship with an unbeliever (session 2, question 9)? If so, what happened? If not, what do you think got in your way? *Erika*

In either case, what thoughts and feelings do you have about this experience?

Understanding how the gospel expanded in the early church can address the decision Mary is facing. The book of Acts illustrates three different but complementary approaches to spreading the gospel: natural expansion, the apostolic team, and local expansion.

NATURAL EXPANSION

IN ACTS 2–11 we read how the gospel expanded naturally through a prepared group of 120 people who had been with Jesus. Quickly and dramatically, the crowd gathered in Jerusalem for the festival of Pentecost responded to their preaching of the gospel. As a result, the lives of these new converts became visible and attractive to the rest of the people in the city. Perhaps all of this growth would have remained within the walls of Jerusalem had it not been for the persecution that accompanied the stoning of Stephen (see Acts 7:54-60).

Acts 11:19 describes what happened as these people spread throughout the regions surrounding Jerusalem. They reached Aramaic-speaking Jews and Jews who had adopted the Greek language and customs. Although the gospel was advancing geographically, it was still (with a few key exceptions) confined culturally—Jews reaching Jews.

THE APOSTOLIC TEAM

THE GREEK WORD *apostle* means "sent one." The New Testament defines the original eleven disciples plus Matthias as apostles. In this sense it was a unique role for a unique period. However, Scripture also extends the title to other "sent ones," including Paul and Barnabas. These apostles traveled across the Roman

Empire with small teams of comrades to plant the gospel in the great cities of the day. They took time to nurture the initial fruit of local believers. A beachhead was established—a foundation generation formed. Then the apostolic team left town and relied on those local believers to carry the gospel deeper into their cities through their households and relational networks. This deeper penetration required approaches other than the apostolic team.

It is the same today! Missionaries can enter an unreached society as strangers and establish a beachhead. But unless the new local believers take up the mantle of insiders to their relational networks, the fruit of the missionary effort will be limited.

From the book of Acts and the letters of Paul, we can see that Paul's apostolic/mobile ministry was:

❖ Sent to people geographically distant from Paul's home base.
❖ Sent to those with some background in the Bible (Jews, and Gentiles who had been hanging around synagogues).
❖ Not local—in town for a few weeks or years.
❖ Focused on laying a foundation.
❖ Based on proclaiming or preaching the gospel in order to reap those with prepared hearts.

> **WHAT CHARACTERIZED THE PAULINE APOSTOLIC/MOBILE MINISTRY?**
>
> To research Paul's apostolic/mobile ministry, see Acts 13:1-5,14,44; 14:1; 18:1-6; 1 Corinthians 3:10-11; 9:19-22; 2 Corinthians 10:13-16.

THE LOCAL EXPANSION

WHAT HAPPENED AFTER the apostolic team left town? The litmus test of Paul's ministry was what the local believers did with the gospel. On several occasions Paul linked the phrase "not in vain" to his apostolic ministry. He used the Greek word *kenos*. Literally, it means empty. Used figuratively, it means useless, for no purpose, or without effect. Paul wanted to see certain things happen in and through the local believers so he could conclude that his ministry in a city or region had fulfilled its purpose.

2. What did Paul want to see happening in and through local believers? Read Philippians 2:14-16; Romans 12:14-21; 1 Corinthians 5:9-13; and Colossians 4:2-6. Write down your observations.

---

[14]Do everything without complaining or arguing, [15]so that you may become blameless and pure, children of God without fault in a crooked and depraved generation, in which you shine like stars in the universe [16]as you hold out the word of life—in order that I may boast on the day of Christ that I did not run or labor for nothing.

—PHILIPPIANS 2:14-16

[14]Bless those who persecute you; bless and do not curse. [15]Rejoice with those who rejoice; mourn with those who mourn. [16]Live in harmony with one another. Do not be proud, but be willing to associate with people of low position. Do not be conceited. [17]Do not repay anyone evil for evil. Be careful to do what is right in the eyes of everybody. [18]If it is possible, as far as it depends on you, live at peace with everyone. [19]Do not take revenge, my friends, but leave room for God's wrath, for it is written: "It is mine to avenge; I will repay," says the Lord. [20]On the contrary: "If your enemy is hungry, feed him; if he is thirsty, give him something to drink. In doing this, you will heap burning coals on his head." [21]Do not be overcome by evil, but overcome evil with good.

—ROMANS 12:14-21

3. To summarize, choose five words or phrases to describe the local ministry. (You might contrast it with apostolic/mobile ministry.)

See Acts 13:1-5
14:44
14:1
18:1-6
1 Cor 3:10-11
9:19-22
2 Cor 10:13-16

> [9]I have written you in my letter not to associate with sexually immoral people—[10]not at all meaning the people of this world who are immoral, or the greedy and swindlers, or idolaters. In that case you would have to leave this world. [11]But now I am writing you that you must not associate with anyone who calls himself a brother but is sexually immoral or greedy, an idolater or a slanderer, a drunkard or a swindler. With such a man do not even eat. [12]What business is it of mine to judge those outside the church? Are you not to judge those inside? [13]God will judge those outside. "Expel the wicked man from among you."
>
> —1 CORINTHIANS 5:9-13

> [2]Devote yourselves to prayer, being watchful and thankful. [3]And pray for us, too, that God may open a door for our message, [4]so that we may proclaim the mystery of Christ, for which I am in chains. Pray that I may proclaim it clearly, as I should. [5]Be wise in the way you act toward outsiders; make the most of every opportunity. [6]Let your conversation be always full of grace, seasoned with salt, so that you may know how to answer everyone.
>
> —COLOSSIANS 4:2-6

THE INSIDER

THE FIRST GENERATION of believers in Corinth faced many challenges. It was tempting to try to resolve these problems by withdrawing from the immoral society around them. But in 1 Corinthians 7, Paul urged them to remain where they were in their culture.

Are you looking for your calling, wondering what God wants you to do? Paul is saying, "Open your eyes and look! You're surrounded!" Some of your relationships are good, some are bad, but they all have potential for new meaning now that you're a citizen of the kingdom of God. Live out that citizenship; "hold out the word of life" (Philippians 2:16). That's what it means to be an insider!

> For more on Paul's challenge to the Corinthian believers, see *The Insider*, pages 59-61.

The concept of insidership challenges many of our traditional assumptions of ministry:

Traditional Ministry Assumptions	Insider Ministry Assumptions
The ordinary believer has a minor role.	The ordinary believer has a key role.
The ordinary believer is a spectator.	The ordinary believer is a vital participant.
The ordinary believer helps the clergy to minister.	The ordinary believer is a minister.
The clergy must oversee ministry.	The Holy Spirit oversees ministry.
Ministry is for the gifted.	All can play a part.
"Come and help us run our program."	Stay there, minister there.
"I can't minister without a lot of training."	"I can minister right now with what I have."
Success is large numbers.	Starting small is okay.
Ministry inside the church walls is a sign of commitment.	Ministry in the world is the work of the church.

4. Which of the insider ministry assumptions listed are hardest for you to accept? Why?

Which are hard for your church to accept? Why?

5. Reread the story at the beginning of this session. What have you learned in this session that could help Mary decide how to spend the rest of her time at college? For example, how could Mary put Paul's instructions into practice at college?

CASE STUDY

How could Mary do what Jesus taught about kingdom living in the previous session?

6. What have you learned that could help Mary decide how to spend the rest of her life?

> It's not our religious activities we want people to see; it's the grace and mercy that comes from God's love that needs to show.
> —*The Insider*, page 57

7. Look back at question 6 of session 1. What changes, if any, would you like to make in your social life in light of what you have been studying?

An Insider Among Christians

YOU'RE AN INSIDER not only among a unique circle of unbelievers but also among a unique circle of believers. You can multiply your ministry by helping other Christians figure out how to be insiders. You don't have to be an expert. Who is one Christian with whom you could share something you've learned from this workbook?

GROUP EXERCISE

Encourage one another to take another initiative of kingdom living this week. How could you do what Paul or Jesus taught? Share the name of an unbeliever in your life and ask the group to pray for you as you seek to show kindness, forgiveness, or some other kingdom trait to that person.

Or, plan some casual social time. Have dinner with an unbelieving individual or couple you know, perhaps along with an individual or couple in your group.

"BUT WHAT IF. . . ?"

From Fear to Freedom

God doesn't want us to be shy with his gifts,
but bold and loving and sensible.
—2 TIMOTHY 1:7, MSG

✳   ✳   ✳

Jeanne, a young Christian teacher, is in her first teaching job in a public school. It's clear to her that she is in an environment somewhat hostile and cynical toward evangelical Christianity. How does she feel? What does she do?

Steve and Linda, a Christian couple, live next door to a couple whose marriage is falling apart. Steve and Linda are nice and polite, but they remain uninvolved. Why? What are they feeling? What could they do?

Gary, a Christian businessman, has just finished a business lunch with Matt, a client Gary has worked with for the past year. Matt is a hard-drinking, party-loving guy who is in the middle of a divorce. Matt has noticed that Gary is different. He doesn't seem to get stressed out and anxious, even when deadlines are approaching and problems are still to be resolved. Matt asks Gary for his secret. Gary wants to say it's prayer and his faith in Christ, but instead he mumbles something about temperament and time management.

> ## *The* INSIDER
>
> Along with this session, read the introduction to part two and chapters 7 and 10 of *The Insider.*
>
> What questions does this reading raise?

1. In what ways do you identify with Jeanne, Steve, Linda, or Gary?

Each of the people in these three scenarios has at least two things in common.

First, all experience fear of one sort or another. Jeanne chooses to remain "incognito" as a believer at school. She fears being typecast as part of the religious right. She's afraid of being intentional in a culture of tolerance. She wants to fit in and fears rejection.

Why are Steve and Linda choosing to remain uninvolved? They fear that involvement will make them lose control of their time and comfort. Also, their own marriage is struggling. What do they have to offer? They are afraid they're inadequate. They fear that their shortcomings will be exposed. After all, what kind of witness would they have if they don't "have it all together" first?

And Gary? He is afraid of saying the wrong thing or not knowing how to answer a difficult question. He's been to several evangelism training seminars that focused on apologetics and presenting the gospel, but he's tried those techniques before and they didn't work. He has offended people, and he doesn't want to repeat the same mistake and lose rapport with his client.

Second, the people in these scenarios are not only experiencing fear; they are paralyzed and controlled by their fears. Fear has the potential to govern our behavior in powerful ways. Some fears are helpful—it's reasonable for a recovering drug addict to fear that contact with his old drug-using friends may lead him astray. However, fear can also cause us to act in ways we know to be wrong or not to act in ways we know to be right.

How did fear govern the behavior of people in Numbers 13:1-3,26-33; 14:1-4? How did fear govern what Peter did in Galatians 2:11-14?

2. When you think of intentionally living as an insider among your unbelieving family, friends, neighbors, and work associates, what fears do you have?

Consider the list below and add any other fears that may apply to you.

☐ Being rejected

☐ Exposing your inadequacy in talking about the gospel

☐ Exposing your own feelings

☐ Exposing the flaws in yourself or your spiritual life

☐ Saying the wrong thing

☐ Being typecast and labeled

☐ Losing friendship

☐ Failing

☐ Adding more stress to your busy life

☐ Negatively affecting your family by involving them with the unbelieving culture

☐ Being contaminated or losing holiness

☐ Living outside your comfort zone

☐ Fearing other Christians' disapproval

☐ _____

☐ _____

☐ _____

3. In what ways do these fears govern your actions?

What Do We Do with Our Fears?

WE ALL EXPERIENCE fears. Fears are not abnormal or wrong. It is not the absence of fear but our response to fear that is crucial. God asks and enables us to move from fear to faith in our relationships with unbelievers. Either we can be paralyzed by our fears, or we can embrace them and allow them to bring us closer to God. With his

²³On their release, Peter and John went back to their own people and reported all that the chief priests and elders had said to them. ²⁴When they heard this, they raised their voices together in prayer to God. "Sovereign Lord," they said, "you made the heaven and the earth and the sea, and everything in them. ²⁵You spoke by the Holy Spirit through the mouth of your servant, our father David:

" 'Why do the nations rage
and the peoples plot in vain?
²⁶The kings of the earth take their stand
and the rulers gather together
against the Lord
and against his Anointed One.'
²⁷Indeed Herod and Pontius Pilate met together with the Gentiles and the people of Israel in this city to conspire against your holy servant Jesus, whom you anointed. ²⁸They did what your power and will had decided beforehand should happen. ²⁹Now, Lord, consider their threats and enable your servants to speak your word with great boldness. ³⁰Stretch out your hand to heal and perform miraculous signs and wonders through the name of your holy servant Jesus." ³¹After they prayed, the place where they were meeting was shaken. And they were all filled with the Holy Spirit and spoke the word of God boldly.

—ACTS 4:23-31

help we can move through fears to a place of obedience and boldness.

The reality of fear in living as an insider raises several questions:

❖ How do we overcome our fears?
❖ How can we develop boldness?
❖ What might boldness look like for the insider?

The Scriptures provide a great deal of counsel on how to overcome fear:

❖ Bring your fears out of the shadows and into the light. Go public with them! Pray over them alone and with others (see Acts 4:23-31; Philippians 1:19-26; 1 John 1:7).

❖ Ask God to deliver you from your fears (see Psalm 34:4).

❖ Ask God to show you which of your fears are wise and which are not (see James 1:5-7).

❖ Eclipse your fears with the fear of the Lord (see Isaiah 6:1-12).

❖ Ask God for the words to say (see Ephesians 6:19-20). We'll look at this in depth in session 8.

❖ Embrace your fears and allow them to take you to deeper dependence on God (see 1 Corinthians 2:1-5; 2 Corinthians 12:1-9).

4. Think about these ways of overcoming fear. Read a few of the related Scripture passages. Which responses to fear do you expect would be most helpful to you?

19For I know that through your prayers and the help given by the Spirit of Jesus Christ, what has happened to me will turn out for my deliverance. 20I eagerly expect and hope that I will in no way be ashamed, but will have sufficient courage so that now as always Christ will be exalted in my body, whether by life or by death. 21For to me, to live is Christ and to die is gain. 22If I am to go on living in the body, this will mean fruitful labor for me. Yet what shall I choose? I do not know! 23I am torn between the two: I desire to depart and be with Christ, which is better by far; 24but it is more necessary for you that I remain in the body. 25Convinced of this, I know that I will remain, and I will continue with all of you for your progress and joy in the faith, 26so that through my being with you again your joy in Christ Jesus will overflow on account of me.

—PHILIPPIANS 1:19-26

4I sought the LORD, and he answered me;
he delivered me from all my fears.

—PSALM 34:4

1When I came to you, brothers, I did not come with eloquence or superior wisdom as I proclaimed to you the testimony about God. 2For I resolved to know nothing while I was with you except Jesus Christ and him crucified. 3I came to you in weakness and fear, and with much trembling. 4My message and my preaching were not with wise and persuasive words, but with a demonstration of the Spirit's power, 5so that your faith might not rest on men's wisdom, but on God's power.

—1 CORINTHIANS 2:1-5

7To keep me from becoming conceited because of these surpassingly great revelations, there was given me a thorn in my flesh, a messenger of Satan, to torment me. 8Three times I pleaded with the Lord to take it away from me. 9But he said to me, "My grace is sufficient for you, for my power is made perfect in weakness." Therefore I will boast all the more gladly about my weaknesses, so that Christ's power may rest on me.

—2 CORINTHIANS 12:7-9

Which responses to fear do you resist? Why is that?

Have you tried any of these responses to fear? If so, what happened?

ONLY JARS OF CLAY WILL SERVE

We have this treasure in jars of clay to show that this all-surpassing power is from God and not from us.
—2 CORINTHIANS 4:7

That is why the jar is best made of clay. Jars of clay do a better job of revealing the treasure they contain than do jars made of finer material. Clay jars are common. They don't distract attention from the contents. There is no confusion about the source of the power. We reveal the reality of the transforming power of the gospel best when we are authentic, honest, and open about our weaknesses.

A friend from Becky's college days came to visit. She was dismissive of the gospel Becky and her husband, Don, had shared in the course of her visit. Then, on the evening before she left, Don and Becky were in tension with each other over something that had happened between the two of them. They were discouraged after they said goodbye to her. They felt they had blown it. Their words seemed to have had no effect and then they had topped off the visit with a petty disagreement between them.

Much to their surprise, the friend phoned a week later to tell them she had become a Christian. She explained that it was the way they had handled the disagreement that had captured her attention. She had seen how both of them had felt pain rather than going to war over their difference. *What kind of a relationship is this?* she asked herself. *What makes it work?* "Then," she said, "I realized the connection between the things you were telling me and the way you live your lives."

They had revealed Christ to her through their weakness. She could identify with that! She knew *she* was made of clay. It gave her hope to discover Don and Becky were made of the same stuff.

—*THE INSIDER*, PAGES 139-140

5. What weaknesses in your life do you most want to hide from unbelievers?

Look again at 1 Corinthians 2:1-5 and 2 Corinthians 12:1-9. How do you respond to the idea that God will be revealed most clearly through your weaknesses?

6. What is one situation in which you feel afraid to live as an insider?

What do you fear might happen in that situation?

What do you think God would like you to do?

7. What step can you take this week toward overcoming a fear related to insidership?

BOLDNESS WITH RAPPORT

WHEN WE THINK of boldness in sharing the gospel, we often think of words such as:

- ❖ *Abrasive*
- ❖ *Proclaiming strongly*
- ❖ *Intrusive*
- ❖ *Dominating*

These are not attractive words for the insider. Relationships and rapport are vital to him or her. They are the tracks down which the gospel travels. Rapport says, "I want to hear what you have to say. I am listening." People stop listening when we pass the level of rapport they feel with us.

We have a dilemma. Abrasive, intrusive boldness will cost us relationship. Yet relationship without boldness won't provide access for the gospel either. It takes words to bring someone to Christ. We need to be bold. Jesus was bold, and the people who followed him picked it up.

So what does boldness look like in the midst of ongoing relationships? Boldness is depending on the Holy Spirit as we take the initiative—through word or action—to help a person move forward in the process of coming to Christ.

BOLDNESS IN LOVING PEOPLE

Boldness is not always expressed in words. Jim's wife, Marge, is at home with people she has never seen before. Conversations flow around her. She has a boldness that creates rapport because it comes out of a natural interest in people. She is quick to serve a total stranger in some little way, like helping the person get an arm into a coat. She has no agenda. Boldness in loving people is always appropriate. Jim has learned from her that when he's bold in acting out of love for people, the right words follow much more easily. Insiders need to learn to be bold in ways that enhance rapport. The apostle Paul wrote, "Use your heads as you live and work among outsiders. Don't miss a trick. Make the most of every opportunity. Be gracious in your speech. The goal is to bring out the best in others in a conversation, not put them down, or cut them out" (Colossians 4:5-6, MSG).

8. The illustration on page 22 depicts the process of evangelism. Imagine that you have a coworker named Andrew who is early in the process—he is hostile to the gospel. He criticizes Christians for being intolerant of diverse beliefs. What would boldness look like in your relationship with Andrew?

9. Now imagine that you're on the board of your homeowner's association. Lisa, the board chairwoman, seems indifferent to spiritual things. What would boldness look like in your relationship with Lisa?

CASE STUDY

Choose one of the scenarios from the beginning of this session. What would boldness look like:

- ☐ For Jeanne?
- ☐ For Steve and Linda?
- ☐ For Gary?

Boldness involves life first. It means letting people really get to know us. The gospel is seen not in our perfection but in the reality of all our humanity. Paul describes the Corinthians (who were not perfect!) as "a letter from Christ" (2 Corinthians 3:3). Their lives were the message. Words on paper may or may not be genuine, but a life observed over time — that's different. Take the risk to let unbelievers really get to know you.

Boldness also involves words. Boldness means being willing to "converse" about the life, death, and resurrection of Christ, our relationship with him, and what it means to surrender to him. This is like the signature on the letter of our lives. We need to develop the skills of conversation more than proclamation. It is around the dinner table, in the boardroom, and at the barbeque that we need to be able to speak words of grace. (We will look more at conversing about the faith in session 9.)

If you only look at *us*, you might well miss the brightness. We carry this precious Message around in the unadorned clay pots of our ordinary lives. That's to prevent anyone from confusing God's incomparable power with us.

—2 CORINTHIANS 4:7, MSG

He told me, "My grace is enough; it's all you need. My strength comes into its own in your weakness." Once I heard that, I was glad to let it happen. I quit focusing on the handicap and began appreciating the gift. It was a case of Christ's strength moving in on my weakness.

—2 CORINTHIANS 12:9, MSG

10. Finally, imagine that Ellen, the mother of one of your child's friends, is interested in spiritual things but knows little about what Jesus actually did and taught. What would boldness look like in your relationship with Ellen?

11. Consider the fears you noted in question 2. What will boldness look like for you as you go beyond this fear? What is something bold you could do to enhance your rapport with an unbeliever?

GROUP EXERCISE

Share with one another your fears and your desires for boldness. Then pray for one another using ideas from the Scriptures on pages 34-35.

"I Can't Do That!"

From Isolation to Freedom

Christ has set us free to live a free life. So take your stand!
Never again let anyone put a harness of slavery on you.
—GALATIANS 5:1, MSG

❋   ❋   ❋

Ian and Emily have given their lives to Christ. They have a consistent devotional life, memorize and study Scripture, and faithfully attend church. Once a month they take part in a program distributing tracts and invitations for their church in a new neighborhood near their own. Yet Ian and Emily have no meaningful involvement with unbelievers either at their work or in their neighborhood. Why is this?

> ### *The* INSIDER
>
> Along with this session, read chapter 8 of *The Insider.*
>
> What questions does this reading raise?

There may be a number of reasons, but an obvious one is that they both hold very strong personal convictions about not drinking alcohol. Their convictions have created a dilemma for them. What if they asked their friends over for a barbeque, and their friends brought some wine! What then? What would their children think of alcohol in the house? What if some of their Christian friends were to visit during the barbeque? What would they think? Ian and Emily can think of some who would be deeply offended. It's all too complicated for Ian and Emily. So they withdraw from relational involvement and instead share the gospel by putting tracts into anonymous mailboxes.

Pete is a lawyer in a growing and prestigious law firm. He became a Christian while at college. He longs to live out his Christian life within the firm. Each Friday afternoon many of the lawyers gather for a meal and then play poker. It's a chance to unwind at the end of the week and talk about things other than caseloads. Pete has joined in on this fun time. However, the only other Christian in the firm has approached Pete and made it clear he does not approve of Pete's actions. He told Pete he was compromising by taking part in gambling.

Pete too has a dilemma. He can continue to relate freely Friday after work and offend his fellow Christian, or he can avoid offending the Christian and risk sending a distorted message to his fellow lawyers about what it means to follow Jesus.

Ian and Emily and Pete are in different situations, but both situations involve issues that, if not addressed, will severely limit their freedom to live as insiders. For Ian and Emily, the issue is how to relate to their unbelieving neighbors without offending their own consciences on what is right and wrong. For Pete, the issue is what other Christians will think. Pete does not have a problem with playing cards, but others do. They will be offended. What should Pete do?

Unfortunately, people usually don't respond to these issues biblically. When they don't, people like Ian, Emily, and Pete withdraw into the safety of evangelistic programs that bypass involvement with unbelievers as the living presence of Christ in their midst. They have added to the numbers who live in a Christian ghetto within the walls of legalism.

What do we do about this? Should we curb our freedom to appease fellow Christians and risk confusing our unbelieving friends concerning the purity of the gospel? Or do we honor our believing friends and modify our behavior accordingly? How can we tell the difference between godly restraint and legalism? These are not easy issues to resolve.

1. Do you identify with Ian, Emily, or Pete in any way? What is one situation that raises the conscience question for you?

Step 1: Is This a Disputable Matter?

THE SCRIPTURES IDENTIFY three types of behavior. There are behaviors that are always right, some that are always wrong, and "disputable matters"—matters that are right or wrong depending on the context.

In Galatians 5:19-21, Paul gives us a summary of behaviors that are always wrong. He follows this with a description of behaviors that are always right; behaviors that fit everywhere, in whatever culture. He used the term "disputable matters" (see Romans 14:1-5) to refer to questions of behavior not specifically addressed in Scripture.

The list of disputable matters shifts constantly as our culture changes. Over the centuries everything from wearing colored clothing to sleeping on a soft bed has had its turn on the list. When we look back, yesterday's list of disputable matters always seems so quaint. But people defend their lists with zeal. It's as if they were defending the faith itself!

2. Give one example of a behavior with an unbeliever that would always be right. *example: Helping to provide meals when the family cook is ill.*

> [19]The acts of the sinful nature are obvious: sexual immorality, impurity and debauchery; [20]idolatry and witchcraft; hatred, discord, jealousy, fits of rage, selfish ambition, dissensions, factions [21]and envy; drunkenness, orgies, and the like. I warn you, as I did before, that those who live like this will not inherit the kingdom of God.
> —GALATIANS 5:19-21
>
> [22]But the fruit of the Spirit is love, joy, peace, patience, kindness, goodness, faithfulness, [23]gentleness and self-control. Against such things there is no law.
> —GALATIANS 5:22-23
>
> [1]Accept him whose faith is weak, without passing judgment on disputable matters. [2]One man's faith allows him to eat everything, but another man, whose faith is weak, eats only vegetables. [3]The man who eats everything must not look down on him who does not, and the man who does not eat everything must not condemn the man who does, for God has accepted him. [4]Who are you to judge someone else's servant? To his own master he stands or falls. And he will stand, for the Lord is able to make him stand. [5]One man considers one day more sacred than another; another man considers every day alike. Each one should be fully convinced in his own mind.
> —ROMANS 14:1-5

Give one example of a behavior with an unbeliever that would always be wrong. *example: Talking about how much you hate the neighbor across the street.*

3. Disputable behaviors are the things the Bible doesn't address specifically. We have to form our own convictions in these areas. What issues do believers dispute today?

STEP 2: FORM YOUR OWN CONVICTIONS

THE EARLY CHRISTIANS constantly had to make decisions about disputable matters. To help them form convictions about these matters, Paul framed two principles: the law of love and the law of self-control.

The Laws of Love and Self-control

According to Romans 13:8-10, deciding about a disputable matter looks obvious. All we need to do is ask, How, in this situation, do I show love to this person? When we show love, most of the time we can assume we have made the right choice.

Most of the time, but not always. We also need to ask, Can I, personally, handle this choice? A recovering drug addict may find that he would risk temptations he could not handle if he set out to be an insider among his drug pals. Those relationships would not be beneficial (see 1 Corinthians 6:12). He would risk being mastered by something.

A college student who is not inclined to be a

> [8]He who loves his fellowman has fulfilled the law. [9]The commandments, "Do not commit adultery," "Do not murder," "Do not steal," "Do not covet," and whatever other commandment there may be, are summed up in this one rule: "Love your neighbor as yourself." [10]Love does no harm to its neighbor. Therefore love is the fulfillment of the law.
> —ROMANS 13:8-10

> "Everything is permissible for me"—but not everything is beneficial. "Everything is permissible for me"—but I will not be mastered by anything.
> —I CORINTHIANS 6:12

> [24]Do you not know that in a race all the runners run, but only one gets the prize? Run in such a way as to get the prize. [25]Everyone who competes in the games goes into strict training. They do it to get a crown that will not last; but we do it to get a crown that will last forever. [26]Therefore I do not run like a man running aimlessly; I do not fight like a man beating the air. [27]No, I beat my body and make it my slave so that after I have preached to others, I myself will not be disqualified for the prize.
> —I CORINTHIANS 9:24-27

binge drinker or sexually promiscuous might be able to hang out at wild parties, while another who still feels drawn to those behaviors might need to find other settings in which to see his old friends.

The gospel is the good news about freedom. "It is for freedom that Christ has set us free," Paul writes. "Stand firm, then, and do not let yourselves be burdened again by a yoke of slavery" (Galatians 5:1). Love sets us free to do what we can handle, and self-control frees us from the things we can't handle.

4. Imagine you're building a relationship with your neighbor, Erik. You both play golf. It makes sense to go golfing together. But you know that after you go golfing at his club, Erik will want to go to the clubhouse for a whiskey. What will you do? How will you apply love and self-control?

STEP 3: AVOID LEGALISM

Are you so foolish? After beginning with the Spirit,
are you now trying to attain your goal by human effort?
—GALATIANS 3:3

In giving his lists of always right/always wrong in Galatians 5:19-23, Paul wasn't asking us to pin them on our wall and set out to keep them. We would utterly fail. Instead of giving a list to keep, Paul was describing what we can expect the Holy Spirit to do in us. There is a world of difference between submitting to the Holy Spirit and submitting to human regulations. Fruit of the Spirit comes from him! It is the outworking of his inner workings in us. The effects on those who are watching are equally distinct. True transformation from within baffles those who know us best. They can't believe we've actually changed. The wonder of it draws the observer to look more closely. But when our religion comes across as a set of rules we are following and trying to impose on others, people flee!

Creating lists of rules people have to keep is called legalism. Legalism is confusing human rules with the clear teaching of Scripture. We become legalistic whenever we:

❖ Universalize a personal conviction. ("I can't do this and neither should you." "I must do this and so must you.")
  examples:

  • "I have chosen not to shop on Sunday and neither should any other Christian."
  • "We homeschool and so should all Christians."
  • "We don't allow our children to have body piercings and neither should other Christian parents."

❖ Make a good idea or form normative for everyone.
  examples:

  • Everyone must have a devotional time in the morning.
  • Everyone must use verse cards to memorize Scripture.

❖ Universalize not only clear teaching about what is right to do, but also the application.
  example:

  • The Bible says we should not neglect to meet together, but encourage each other daily. Therefore everyone must attend at least one worship service each Sunday.

Legalism harms believers by:

  ❖ Hindering a life rooted in faith rather than lists of rules—(see Mark 7:1-23).
  ❖ Hindering unity—(see Romans 14).
  ❖ Stunting the growth to maturity that comes through the power of the Holy Spirit (believers bypass the deep work of transformation and settle

for mere reformation or religious conformity)—(see 1 Corinthians 8–10; Colossians 2; and Hebrews 5:11-14).

Legalism harms unbelievers by:

> **AN INSIDER AMONG CHRISTIANS**
>
> Tell a friend something you've learned about dealing with fear or legalism.

❖ Hindering the mobility of the gospel—(see Acts 15).

❖ Alienating unbelievers—(see Matthew 23:13-14).

5. Consider your life and response to Christians before you became a believer. Or if you grew up in a Christian home, think about your life as a young person. What impact did Christian legalism have on your understanding of who Jesus is and what being a follower of him looks like?

What impact, if any, does legalism still have on your relationship with Jesus and your concept of following him?

STEP 4: DECIDE WHOM TO PLEASE

THE BIBLE DISTINGUISHES four kinds of people and how we are to relate to them in this area of disputable matters:

❖ the unbeliever—he needs to see a gospel without legalism;

❖ the new believer—he might be tempted to violate his conscience;

❖ the weak believer—he won't be tempted to violate his conscience, but he's inclined to judge you for your behavior on disputable matters; and

❖ the mature believer—he won't be tempted, and he won't judge you.

When deciding what to do about a disputable matter, we should consider the unbeliever's and new believer's consciences carefully. We shouldn't be concerned with the weak believer's judgment.

FOR FURTHER STUDY

If you want to study the four kinds of people—and our response to them—more deeply, see Romans 14:1-23; 1 Corinthians 8:1-13; 9:19-23; 10:23-33; Galatians 2:11-14; and Hebrews 5:11-14. See also *The Insider*, chapter 8.

6. Imagine you play golf with Erik. Then you go to his clubhouse. A friend of yours from church walks in. You know he feels strongly that Christians should not drink alcohol or associate with those who, like Erik, drink quite a bit. What do you do?

7. What questions and concerns do you still have about forming convictions and resisting legalism?

CASE STUDY

What have you learned in this session that could help Ian and Emily, whose story began this session? What counsel would you give them?

What counsel would you give Pete?

"BUT I DON'T HAVE TIME."

From Busyness to Margin

*Don't become so well-adjusted to your
culture that you fit into it without
even thinking.*

—ROMANS 12:2, MSG

＊　　＊　　＊

Jennifer works thirty hours a week as a hairdresser. Her husband, Bruce, is an engineer with a consulting firm. Consultants have to hustle or they don't get the contract. Bruce is convinced that if he doesn't work sixty hours a week, his job is in jeopardy.

Bruce and Jennifer have two daughters—ages ten and

> ### *The* INSIDER
>
> **Along with this session, read chapter 9 of *The Insider*.**
>
> **What questions does this reading raise?**

thirteen—who are both in city league soccer with practices twice a week and games on the weekends. Their home is twenty-five years old and needs mainte-nance. Between the house, two active daughters, and their jobs, Bruce and Jennifer are stretched thin. Their extended family lives all over the country. They have friends from church, but busy lives keep them and their friends from spend-ing a lot of time together. Their church friends don't know their work associates. The families from the girls' soccer leagues are another completely separate circle of acquaintances. The same is true with the girls' school friends. And they don't even know most of their neighbors' names.

THE PAIN OF PROGRESS[4]

The average American:
- Lives virtually on an island of independent and private pursuits.
- Is too busy.
- Has life divided into compartments—work, family, fun, church—that often involve completely different relationships, conflicting expectations, and competing priorities.
- Experiences a profound loss of meaning.
- Feels squeezed on all sides and doesn't know how to get out.

The idea of progress holds that humanity has advanced in the past, is now advancing, and will continue to advance through the foreseeable future. Economics, education, and technology have tapped into our drives to have more, know more, and do more. Collectively, we now have more houses, cars, clothes, TVs, CD players, and computers than ever before. We have more information to assimilate and can build things faster, better, and stronger than ever before.

But for all of these gains, we have paid a great price. We have succumbed to the tendency to inexorably add detail to our lives: one more option, one more problem, one more commitment, one more expectation, one more purchase, one more debt, one more change. We feel like we are on the fast track to exhaustion and collapse.

The greatest price lies in the area of relationships. Instead of loving more, some are finding it difficult to love at all. Their relationship with God seems distant and lifeless. Socially, they feel isolated or in conflict. Personally, they feel anxious and stressed.

We know this busyness and fragmentation all too well. But are we aware of how negatively this cultural reality affects the flow of the gospel? How available are we to love and form meaningful relationships with the people we live among? Is the light of Christ visible to the unbelieving world in the compartmentalized, insular, busy life we lead?

Margin "is the space between our load and our limits"[5]; something held in reserve for contingencies or unexpected situations; the gap between rest and exhaustion, between reacting and choosing, between survival and living purposely. *Integration* means synthesis, unity, the combination or coordination of separate elements of life so as to provide a harmonious, interrelated whole. If we have no margin, we are too drained to be God's presence in the world. Without integration, we are too scattered to invest in key relationships. We need to be visible to unbelievers if they are to catch a glimpse of Christ through us.

When Jennifer and Bruce hear the call to be insiders, they say, "We wish we could, but we don't have time." When someone exhorts them to simplify their lives, they think, "Sure. Sounds great. What do you have in mind? Should we pull the kids out of soccer and deny them the benefits of such activities? Should we downsize to a smaller house and force our thirteen-year-old to share a bedroom with her sister? Are there low-stress, well-paid jobs out there that somebody forgot to tell us about?"

1. What obstacles do Jennifer and Bruce face if they want to live as insiders?

2. In what ways can you identify with the stressed and fragmented life described in "The Pain of Progress"?

What can we do to regain the margin, integration, and visibility that are essential to the gospel's advance through our lives? We can learn a great deal from the example of the early Christians.

THE EARLY CHURCH

IN THE GRECO-ROMAN world, the household (Greek: *oikos*) was the basic unit of society. A person lived, worked, relaxed, and worshiped with the same small network of people. These existing relationships became the vehicle that carried the gospel into the culture of the first century. New life in Christ was lived out in the *oikos* among all the relationships the person already had when he or she became a Christian.

Contrast that with our fragmented lives today, in which too often Christianity is another fragment in an already fragmented life.

> **FOR FURTHER STUDY**
>
> To study how the household (*oikos*) was the setting for the gospel's spread in the first century, see Acts 11:13-14; 16:14-15; 16:31-34; 18:7-8; 20:20; 1 Corinthians 16:15; and Philippians 4:22.

3. In the New Testament, church (*ekklesia*) was inseparable from family, economic, and social life (*oikos*). The early church did not create new structures. Rather, it transformed the existing forms and relationships. The gospel flowed from household to household.

In what ways might the integration of the household (*oikos*) and church (*ekklesia*) have affected:

The individual believer?

The unbelieving world?

The Challenge We Face

OBVIOUSLY, WE SHOULD not attempt to live in the twenty-first century as if it were the first. However, some important implications emerge from the New Testament example.

- ❖ Once planted, the gospel flowed through existing relational networks. This meant the transforming power of the gospel was very visible to the unbelieving world.
- ❖ The integration of church and household meant that church was visible and integrated with life. People didn't have to go to the church; it was in their midst.

By contrast, our contemporary social structure segments our relationships into compartments. We have a family life; we're expected to keep that to ourselves. Our business environments require another behavior. Social relationships often have no connection to either family or business. Churches split up families at the front door so they can go to their appropriate classes.

For many people, believers and unbelievers, our contemporary equivalent to the *oikos* (household) of the New Testament can be illustrated as a set of independent institutions:

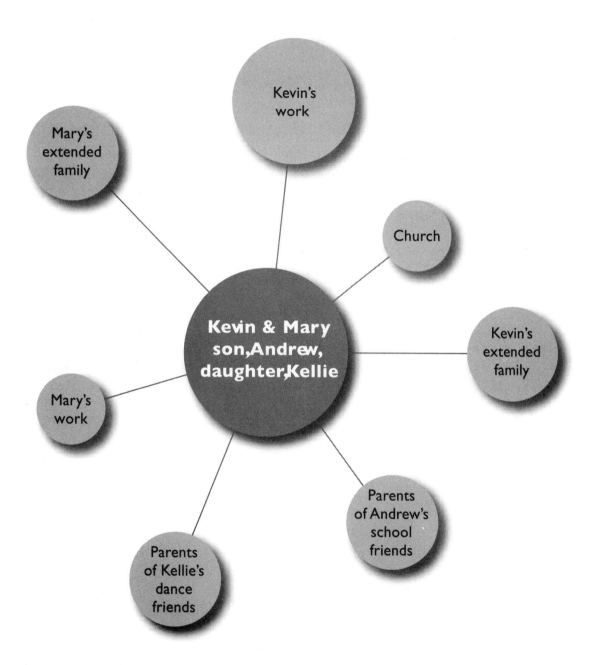

4. In the space following, use your imagination and draw a picture that illustrates how your life and relationships are currently arranged. Add names. Who would you include in your *oikos* (social network; circle of friends, family, and associates)?

5. What does your illustration tell you about the way you are currently living?

Is your life too fragmented? Too insular? Are your relationships too diffuse? Are you trying to do too much?

If you answered yes anywhere in question 5, you need to give up some things you never should have taken on and take back the things you never should have given away. Ouch! That's not easy for any of us to do. It's easy to say, "I should be working fewer hours" or "I spend too much time driving kids to sports." But to cut back at work or with kids' activities has a real, tangible cost. That's where most of us give up: we see the cost, judge it to be too high, and go back to our overloaded, fragmented lives. We need to take some time to contemplate the cost of making changes compared to *the cost of not making changes.*

6. If you wanted to reduce your overload so that your life was less stressed, what sacrifices would you have to make in the areas of:

❖ Having more?

❖ Doing more?

❖ Knowing more?

GROUP EXERCISE

The picture you drew of your existing relational network is the most natural place for your focus as an insider. That is your unique *oikos*. You don't need to go somewhere else to find a place to minister. You don't need to take on new relationships. Your sphere of ministry is all around you. Therefore, ministry doesn't need to be an added task on an already overloaded calendar.

Have each person in the group (who wants to) share the picture of his or her current way of living. Talk about the picture as a group. Here are some questions to think about:

- What is going well and can be strengthened? That is, in what relationships are you already showing care for people? What foundations for relationship have already been laid?

- To what extent is your relational world fragmented into separate compartments? What can you do to integrate your life so that you have fewer separate compartments to deal with?

- Which relationships do you want to emphasize? Which ones can you de-emphasize?

- What changes do you need to make in your relational world? What will those changes cost? What will it cost if you decide *not* to make those changes?

- Who and what is important to you? Who and what gets your attention?

A WORLD OF CHOICES

There is no one-size-fits-all script for integrating our lives so we can give attention to relationships with unbelievers. Here are some choices various people are making:

- Gil and Julia have a daughter who is passionate about gymnastics. They have had to weigh the costs and value of supporting their daughter in an athletic pursuit that will consume lots of family time. They have decided that the families of their daughter's teammates are their insider network. Gil and Julia have recruited another Christian couple with a gymnast daughter to share the effort. They open their home to host team parties and informal gatherings. They watch for opportunities to serve other families and show an interest in their life struggles. They pray for the Holy Spirit's guidance in handling both competitive losses and triumphs gracefully, encouraging the other kids, and helping their daughter avoid the eating disorders and other traps common among gymnasts. Gil and Julia don't have time to volunteer at church or pursue their own hobbies—they know that for a decade, the gymnastics world will be their world.

- Mimi graduated from college with a degree in journalism, and she chose to work in a secular newsroom rather than in Christian media because she wanted to be an insider in that world. She has had to find a handful of Christian friends to support her because she doesn't have time to attend church singles events or other Christian social activities. Spending so much time among unbelieving reporters doesn't give her much opportunity to find a Christian husband, but she has decided her marital status will have to be in God's hands.

- Mike travels extensively for his work with a Christian organization. Because he spends so much time away from home and working with Christians, he has decided to invest his discretionary time with his family, a small circle of Christians who are supporting each other as insiders, and his unbelieving neighbors. Other than with his insider partners, Mike has no time to socialize with Christians.

- For Colin and Jessica, money is time. This is Colin's second marriage, so his sons are with Jessica and him only half of the time. Colin is committed to being home and available when the boys are around. His ex-wife isn't a Christian, so being around Colin and Jessica will be the boy's primary opportunity to see how Christ can affect a life. Colin has passed up a promotion at work because it would mean he would have to travel on weekends when the boys are at his house. Jessica has made similar trade-offs with her career because stepmothering requires presence. Because Colin pays child support, he and Jessica live on a tight budget in a small house, but they've decided that the benefit is worth the cost. They thought about surrounding themselves with other Christian families so the boys would have Christian friends. But they decided that involving the boys in their outreach to their neighborhood would have a deeper effect on their characters. They welcome the boys' unbelieving friends into their home and talk to the boys about how to be the kind of friend Jesus would be.

7. Do you feel pressures or expectations that make you resist making these sacrifices? If so, what are the sources of those pressures or expectations? What are those sources saying to you?

CASE STUDY

Look back at the story about Jennifer and Bruce at the beginning of this session. What choices would you suggest Jennifer and Bruce make? What would be the costs and benefits?

---

8. What would motivate you to resist those pressures and expectations?

PERSONAL RETREAT

Look at your calendar. Schedule some time to . . .

☐ Consider what motivates your busyness.

☐ Simplify your lifestyle in order to have more margin.

☐ Create space in your life in order to love people more.

☐ Address those things that drain your emotions the most.

"How Do I Begin?"

Taking Initiatives

* * *

You can't wait to overcome all your fears, isolation, and busyness before you start operating as an insider. The important thing is to start and then deal with obstacles along the way. The rest of this workbook will equip you with life patterns that together add up to formidable insidership. In this session you'll look at two life patterns that are closely linked: taking little initiatives and practicing a life of service.

> ## *The* INSIDER
>
> Along with this session, read chapters 11 and 13 of *The Insider.*
>
> What questions does this reading raise?

God took the initiative and moved into our world as a human being. In speaking of this initiative, the apostle John said, "No one has ever seen God, but God the One and Only, who is at the Father's side, has made him known" (John 1:18). God, who is invisible, became visible. We saw him as he lived among us.

We too can make visible the invisible Christ as we take a range of initiatives with the people who make up our world.

It all boils down to living the way a citizen of God's kingdom would live.

GREET PEOPLE

TAKE THE INITIATIVE to *greet* people—to speak to those you see every day but never say hello to. Whenever you can, greet people by name. Amazingly, Jesus elevated this simple initiative and gave it significance in kingdom living (see Matthew 5:46-48).

1. What role do fear, isolation, and busyness play in your willingness to greet others?

> 46"If you love those who love you, what reward will you get? Are not even the tax collectors doing that? 47And if you greet only your brothers, what are you doing more than others? Do not even pagans do that? 48Be perfect, therefore, as your heavenly Father is perfect."
> —MATTHEW 5:46-48

2. List at least three places where you could greet people. *examples: On the train to work. At the gym.*

3. Learn the names of three people you wouldn't normally greet. Write them here so you'll remember them. Then you'll be able to greet those people by name.

4. Make a point of greeting people for several days. Write down what happens.

Be Different

5. Read the box "Being Different." What are two difficult relationships in which you have an opportunity to treat people "kingdomly"? What can you do to be different in those relationships?

> ### Being Different
>
> Kingdom citizens are just different from the rest. When they realize they have offended someone, they drop whatever they're doing—even if it's worshiping God—and go reconcile with that person. They keep their anger in check. They don't degrade another person by lusting for them. They keep their word, and are generous even toward people who want to take advantage of them. They even love their enemies (see Matthew 5:21-43).

Serve People

TAKE THE INITIATIVE to *serve* people. As you do so, be sure to let people also serve you. Mutuality is an important part of relationships.

6. List at least three opportunities to serve that you encounter. *examples: Nate needed somebody to listen to him. I picked up the slack for my coworker when her son was sick and I didn't make her feel guilty about it.*

7. What happened when you served these people?

IDEAS ON SERVING

- Give people your time. In the parable of the Good Samaritan, what was it in the heart/values of the Levite and priest (see Luke 10:30-37) that enabled them to pass by and not respond to the need? What was in the Samaritan's heart?

- Offer hospitality. In Luke 14:12-24, Jesus encourages us to be like God and invite the outcasts of our culture into our circle of relationships.

- Stop and listen to people.

- Offer the gift of being "fully present."

- Weep with those who weep, and rejoice with those who rejoice (see Romans 12:15).

- Show mercy instead of judgment (see John 8:1-11).

- Speak truth where a lie would be to your advantage.

- Keep your word (see Matthew 5:33-37).

- Keep your anger in check (see Matthew 5:21-22).

- When you realize you've offended someone, drop what you're doing and be reconciled with that person (see Matthew 5:23-24).

- Be generous (see Matthew 5:38-42).

- Treat an enemy with loving care (see Matthew 5:43-47).

---

8. Write down one way in which an unbeliever could serve you. (What help do you need on a small task, such as moving something heavy? Is there a tool or skill or cooking ingredient you could borrow? Is there something a coworker could do for you that he or she would feel good about doing?) Don't wait for the person to offer—take the initiative to ask. And thank them.

9. To whom could you offer the hospitality of a shared meal? Think especially of two or three people you wouldn't usually invite. It doesn't have to be an elaborate feast—you could invite a coworker to lunch or have a neighbor over for pasta.

10. If you find yourself not taking initiatives with people, what do you think are the obstacles? What role does busyness play? What about fear?

LOVING WITHOUT STRINGS ATTACHED

God loves people whether they love him back or not. The farmer who hates God gets just as much sun and rain on his crops as does his neighbor the next farm over, who loves God. Why do the wicked prosper? They prosper because God loves them! Jesus is saying, "You do the same. Love the people in your life without having an agenda for them. Love them because God loves them."

Frequently, someone will ask . . ., "How long should I stick with a friendship? I've been a friend to this person for almost two years and he's no closer to becoming a Christian now than he was when we first met. Should I forget him and move on?" The reply, of course, is, "If that is our agenda in our friendships, if we are interested in people only because of what we might accomplish with them, then we have missed the point. When we think like that, we aren't loving as our heavenly Father does. He loves with no strings attached."

—*THE INSIDER*, PAGE 148

AN INSIDER WITH CHRISTIANS

Share with a friend something you've learned about taking initiatives.

"WHAT IS GOD'S JOB?"

Praying and Responding

*   *   *

On page 10 you made a list of people in your relational network. As you think about these people, the following truths can save you years of frustration:

❖ God was there long before you were.

❖ God is already at work in their hearts.

❖ God wants to use you in their lives.

Those truths can give you confidence to pray for your friends, associates, neighbors, and family. Those truths can also motivate you to be sensitive to what God is doing in a person's life. Your prayers will be most fruitful when you link your prayers to his work. Finally the truths can motivate you not only to pray, but also to be willing to respond with action as God leads.

> ### *The* INSIDER
>
> Along with this session, read chapter 12 of *The Insider*.
>
> **What questions does this reading raise?**

1. Describe your current prayer life for unbelievers. What do you pray? When? Why? What happens?

Several years ago our family moved into a new neighborhood as it was being built up. A new neighborhood offers certain advantages. Because everyone is new to the area and relational lines have not yet been formed, people are especially open to connecting with their neighbors. Soon after we settled in, Marge and I, together with another neighbor, took a little initiative. We wanted to stimulate a sense of community by helping people meet one another. So we organized a neighborhood crime-watch.

Our local police department promotes the organizing of neighborhood crime-watch groups. They provide the orientation and materials for any neighborhood that is interested. We contacted the police department, and one evening a policeman came to our home, where all of our neighbors had gathered for the occasion.

The policeman instructed us to make everyone's name and phone number available to each other in case of emergency. A piece of paper was passed around and we wrote our names and addresses on it. One neighbor took the names. She drew a map of the neighborhood, showing all the houses and streets and the names of everyone living in all the houses. She then mailed a copy of the map to every household.

When our copy arrived in the mail, I realized I had just received my prayer list! I began to use the map in my times alone with God. I would put my finger on a house and pray for the names of the people living in it. Sometimes, because of my frightfully limited attention span when I pray, I would walk through the neighborhood, praying for people as I passed their houses. I found that helped me stay focused.

It's easy to remember people's names when you are praying for them, so it didn't take long for me to know the names of everyone in the neighborhood. When I'd see my neighbor across the cul-de-sac getting into his car, I'd shout a greeting to him: "Hello Dan!"

Surprised at hearing his name, he would look up and shout, "Hi there, how are ya!"

After a few such exchanges he apparently got out his copy of that map. He was ready for me the next time. When I greeted him, he shouted back, "Hi Jim!"

Friendship was imminent from that point on. He had made the effort to learn my name. We both felt good about that.

—JIM PETERSEN, *THE INSIDER*, PAGES 151-152

What did you learn from Jim's example about how to incorporate prayer for unbelievers into your daily routine?

FOR FURTHER STUDY

There are many examples in the Gospels of people approaching Christ on behalf of someone else. Intercessory prayer enables us to do a similar thing for our friends and associates.

In the following passages, note the attitude of those who approached Jesus. Who were they interceding for? Note also how Jesus responds to their intercession.

- Matthew 8:5-13
- Matthew 9:2-6
- Matthew 15:21-28
- Matthew 17:14-20

2. What can we pray for unbelievers? Read the following passages. Below each one, write down the name of any unbeliever who comes to mind, along with how you might pray for that person using that particular passage.

❖ John 3:5-8 (The Spirit goes where he will, giving new birth.)

❖ John 16:7-11 (The Spirit convicts unbelievers that the sin is real and unbelief is the core of sin, that Jesus alone is righteous, and that God will judge every person.)

❖ 1 Thessalonians 1:4-5 (The gospel reached Thessalonica not just with words, but "with power, with the Holy Spirit and with deep conviction.")

3. Jesus' parable of the soils (see Matthew 13:1-23) is another source of ideas for prayer. Prayer breaks up rocks in the soil of a heart so that the seed of the gospel can be planted. Who do you know who could use prayer for a rocky heart?

---

[5]Jesus answered, "I tell you the truth, no one can enter the kingdom of God unless he is born of water and the Spirit. [6]Flesh gives birth to flesh, but the Spirit gives birth to spirit. [7]You should not be surprised at my saying, 'You must be born again.' [8]The wind blows wherever it pleases. You hear its sound, but you cannot tell where it comes from or where it is going. So it is with everyone born of the Spirit."

—JOHN 3:5-8

[7]"But I tell you the truth: It is for your good that I am going away. Unless I go away, the Counselor will not come to you; but if I go, I will send him to you. [8]When he comes, he will convict the world of guilt in regard to sin and righteousness and judgment: [9]in regard to sin, because men do not believe in me; [10]in regard to righteousness, because I am going to the Father, where you can see me no longer; [11]and in regard to judgment, because the prince of this world now stands condemned."

—JOHN 16:7-11

Brothers, my heart's desire and prayer to God for the Israelites is that they may be saved.

—ROMANS 10:1

[4]For we know, brothers loved by God, that he has chosen you, [5]because our gospel came to you not simply with words, but also with power, with the Holy Spirit and with deep conviction. You know how we lived among you for your sake.

—1 THESSALONIANS 1:4-5

Prayer also deals with weeds (like the love of money or success or a drug) that choke the growth of the gospel in someone's life. Who do you know who could use prayer about the weeds in his or her soil?

4. Many have found it helpful to link their prayers to the process of evangelism. Look again at the "Process of Evangelism" illustration on page 22.

Think of three of your friends or associates (use your list on page 10 or your drawing on page 54). Where are they in the process of coming to Christ? Are they still indifferent or antagonistic to the gospel? Are they neutral but ignorant about who Christ is? Do they have the necessary information but resist yielding to Christ's authority in their lives?

Friend 1:

Friend 2:

Friend 3:

GROUP EXERCISE

Use your answers to the questions in this session as the foundation of an extended prayer time in your group. Take turns praying for the unbelievers in your lives.

Consider making prayer for unbelievers a regular feature of your meetings.

5. What can you pray for these people that would move them closer to Christ? Use the following chart to record your response.

Name	What You Are Praying	What Is Happening

> ## LISTENING TO GOD
>
> As we pray, God will guide us. Prayer isn't just talking to God. It's interacting with him. It involves listening. It includes being predisposed to respond to what God puts in our heart.
>
> There are times as I'm praying for someone that I know exactly what I'm supposed to do next. But the idea frightens me. It calls for more boldness than I am comfortable with. The temptation is to shut down and stay where I am—maybe pray a little bit more.
>
> What I need to do at those times is get up, ask for boldness and for the words to go with it, and go do what I'm told. I've done that many times, often with my knees knocking, only to discover God had been there at work, answering my prayers, preparing the way for my doing what he was prompting me to do. . . .
>
> Prayer is a request for the Holy Spirit's active participation in a situation. It brings divine resources to bear on what's going on. . . .
>
> It is also very important to remember the *division of labor* in this work of bringing people into a relationship with Christ. I can't convict anyone of sin, nor can I show someone what true righteousness looks like. I can't make another person realize he is building his life on something that is already doomed. I find, in fact, that when I do get into such subjects, the conversation wears thin very quickly. I begin to sound moralistic. It is better to talk to God about them and ask for the Holy Spirit to do the convincing.
>
> —*The Insider*, pages 154-156

Next time you are together with your group, share with one another what God is doing as you pray.

6. As you pray for your unbelieving friends, listen to any sense you get of how God would like you to respond with action. Write down what you think God wants you to do.

"What Do I Say?"

Conversing the Faith

*   *   *

As a young believer, Mike received training in how to share his faith. "He was taught to tell in just three minutes his story of how he came to faith. He wrote it out and committed it to memory. He also learned to present the gospel in a coherent, concise way. And he learned how to approach strangers, engage them in conversation, and find out if they would be interested in hearing more of what he had to say."[6]

On Sundays, Mike used these skills with strangers at the Botanical Gardens.

Monday through Friday was another story. Mike had gotten a teaching job in an elementary school. He wondered how to apply his newly acquired skills among his fellow teachers. The time never seemed right to interrupt conversations to make a presentation like he had been trained to do. He tried several times, but it didn't go well. This was both frustrating and discouraging. He resorted to asking some of the staff to attend some Christian meetings with him, but no one showed interest. Frustrated and at a loss as to what to do next, Mike began to withdraw socially.[7]

> ### *The* INSIDER
>
> Along with this session, read chapter 14 of *The Insider*.
>
> What questions does this reading raise?

1. Why do you think Mike's efforts to present the gospel to his coworkers were so discouraging?

DEFINITIONS

Conversation—An informal spoken exchange of news and ideas between two or more people.

Conversationalist—A person who is good at or fond of engaging in conversation.

Proclaim—To announce officially or publicly; to declare and indicate clearly; to cry out.

If you were in Mike's situation, what would you do?

---

[4]Pray that I [Paul] may proclaim it [the gospel] clearly, as I should. [5]Be wise in the way you act toward outsiders; make the most of every opportunity. [6]Let your [insiders'] conversation be always full of grace, seasoned with salt, so that you may know how to answer everyone.
—COLOSSIANS 4:4-6

But in your hearts set apart Christ as Lord. Always be prepared to give an answer to everyone who asks you to give the reason for the hope that you have. But do this with gentleness and respect.
—I PETER 3:15

Mike needed to learn how to "converse" his faith with his coworkers. He needed to know how to:

❖ Express spiritual reality in nonreligious language.
❖ Talk about the realities of our shared humanity.
❖ Ask questions that deepen a relationship.
❖ Listen closely to what another person is saying.
❖ Hold a spiritual conversation.

EXPRESSING SPIRITUAL REALITY
IN NONRELIGIOUS LANGUAGE

INSIDERS NEED TO authentically, relevantly, and boldly dialogue about God's work in their lives. This means thinking about how to express spiritual reality in nonreligious language. Three guidelines for doing this are:

❖ Is what I am saying true? (Am I being honest and open?)

❖ Will it make sense to those listening?

❖ Does it create space for dialogue?

For example, you're sitting in the employee lunchroom at your workplace, writing answers in this workbook. Your unbelieving coworker passes by and asks, "What are you reading?" Lying is a bad idea. An answer like, "I'm studying how to share my faith with unbelievers" is true, but it probably will either alienate you or simply not make sense to your coworker. It's a good idea to plan ahead what you'll say so you won't feel embarrassed when the moment comes. Authentic confidence without bravado is the tone you want to set.

Your answer needs to fit you uniquely, but you might say something like, "A lot of Christians are uncomfortable dealing with the world around them so they withdraw into Christian ghettoes. This book is about how Christians can stay engaged with the world even if they don't always agree with how other people do things." Chances are that your coworker is aware that many Christians withdraw and will be interested to hear you being honest about that. Far from making Christians look bad, you're giving your coworker reason to think again about Christians in general and you in particular. You've been vulnerable about a weakness without spilling your guts. He or she might want to pursue the conversation, but even if not, you've left the door open for later.

2. How would you communicate the following scenarios to an unbeliever in nonreligious language? Write out what you would say.

Scenario	What would you say?
Something you are praying about	
How God is helping you with a problem	
What you are reading in the Bible	
What you are learning from the group in discussing this workbook	

It takes some advance planning to think of what to say in situations like these, and many Christians don't want to work that hard. But the alternative is to avoid any conversation that might deal with spiritual reality so that you're never embarrassed.

3. This week, try to share one of your answers from question 2. Record here what happens. What do you learn from this experience?

TALKING ABOUT THE REALITIES OF OUR SHARED HUMANITY

ONE OF THE most powerful ways to relate to an unbeliever is to talk about the realities of our shared humanity. When you do so, emphasize sharing your experience of God, not propositions about God. Focus on talking about the impact of God on areas of common humanity, such as family, career, finances, and so on. As you talk with your friends about life issues such as loneliness, the pain of disappointment, the wounds of broken relationships, and the reality of death, your openness and authenticity will create a safe environment for unbelievers to share their concerns and fears.

To do this, you need to continue to grow in experiencing every aspect of your life.

Learn to use nonreligious language to communicate how a relationship with Jesus makes a difference in those areas. Your goal is to integrate Christian spirituality into your daily life without being religious. In conversations with unbelievers, you want to position Christian faith as a way of living with the power of God, not as a religion. Religion (in the negative sense in which unbelievers often think about it) is about doctrines, rituals, and rules. The gospel is about a Person and a way of living.

The following diagram illustrates Jesus at the center of life, affecting every aspect:

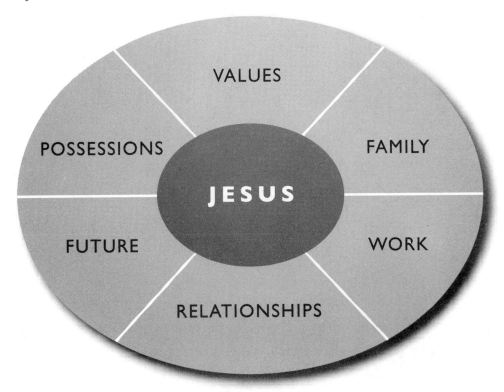

Imagine, for example, that you're standing in a parking lot with a friend, admiring a car there. If you say, "It's just immoral what some people will spend on a car!" you set yourself above others. To converse the faith in an attractive way, you might say, "Boy, do I love cars like that. Kristin and I have agreed that we want to put people ahead of possessions in our lives, but when I look at a car like that, I start scrambling in my head for a way to make the payments." You've now opened the door to have an authentic conversation about the value of people versus possessions. You've been vulnerable, so you don't sound preachy. Further on in this conversation you could say you believe that people are more important because they last forever or even because they reflect God in ways that mechanical stuff can't.

4. Choose one of the topics from the previous diagram. How would you talk to an unbeliever about your experience of God in that area of your life?

Using Questions to Go Deeper

The purposes of a man's heart are deep waters,
but a man of understanding draws them out.

—Proverbs 20:5

ASKING APPROPRIATE QUESTIONS in an atmosphere of love, trust, and acceptance can provide avenues for deeper conversation. What is a good question? Some examples:

Clarifying questions make the current situation, problem, need, or challenge understandable. A couple of examples are: "So are you saying that. . . ?" "What is it about a new car that makes you feel that way?"

Discovery questions promote understanding and awareness. Some examples are:

❖ What do you want to happen?

❖ Say more about that.

❖ What have you already tried?

❖ What are the reasons this didn't go as well as you had hoped?

❖ How do you feel about this?

❖ What are some other choices you could make?

❖ What is the most strategic thing you could do now?

❖ What would need to happen for you to. . . ?

Open-ended questions invite discussion. Examples are:

❖ Tell me more about that.

❖ What are you thinking of doing next?

❖ What are the biggest challenges you face?

Many people have found the book *201 Great Questions*[8] a useful resource in building their ability to ask good questions.

5. Choose two questions from the following list and use them this week at school, in your neighborhood, at work, or with an unbelieving friend. If it seems awkward to launch into a question, tell the person you're doing this for a course you're taking. (Be ready to talk about the course in nonreligious language!) Tell the person his or her response is confidential—you won't share the specific answer in the group. Really listen to the response.

☐ If you didn't have to worry about making a living, what would you most like to do for the rest of your life?

GROUP EXERCISE

Let one participant briefly share a challenging situation he or she is facing. Each of the other participants will suggest two questions he or she could ask to deepen a conversation about the situation. The goal here is to practice coming up with questions in conversation, not to solve the person's problem. It's not necessary for the person to answer the questions.

After each participant has had a chance to pose a couple of questions, talk about the experience. What would have been your typical response to hearing about a challenge like this? Would you normally have offered advice? Shared a similar experience from your own life (thus shifting the focus to yourself)? How easy was it for you to be in question mode? Do you tend to think of questions that feel too intrusive, too shallow, or about right?

- ☐ If you knew tomorrow would be the last full day of your life, how would you spend that day?
- ☐ How would you describe yourself without mentioning anything about what you do for a living?
- ☐ What three things do you believe without any doubts?
- ☐ What is one of the books that has had the greatest influence on your life? Why?
- ☐ What is your favorite movie? Why?
- ☐ Describe a time when you felt real fear. How did you respond?
- ☐ What is the most difficult choice you've had to make in your life up to this point? Why was it difficult?
- ☐ What are three barriers that keep you from reaching your full potential? What would most help you overcome these barriers?
- ☐ Which of your parents has had the greatest influence on your life? How?
- ☐ What living person do you most admire? What person who is no longer living? Why these people?

What did you learn about using questions from your experience asking these?

LISTENING

CONVERSING YOUR FAITH means not only talking but also genuinely listening. Some of us tend to rush in and try to fix things with good advice. We often fail to take time to deeply understand the problem first.

6. Review the following blocks to listening. Check the two with which you most identify.

☐ *Identifying*—You take everything a person tells you and relate it to your own experience. This means you are not giving attention to the other person.

☐ *Sparring*—You debate with people. The other person never feels heard because you are ready with your beliefs and preferences.

☐ *Advising*—You don't have to hear more than a few sentences before you are ready to "fix it."

☐ *Rehearsing*—You don't have time to listen because you are trying to figure out what you are going to say.

☐ *Placating*—You want to be nice, kind, and supportive. You want people to like you, so you are preoccupied with yourself and what you are communicating rather than the other person's story.

☐ *Digressing*—You are half listening, and something the other person says triggers a chain of private associations.

> **GROUP EXERCISE**
>
> Share your answer to question 6 with the others in your group. Ask them to help you make progress in this area. For example, with your permission they might gently let you know when you do one of these listening blocks during group meetings. Would that be okay with you? Or, you might ask the group to pray for you.

HOLDING A SPIRITUAL CONVERSATION

A SPIRITUAL CONVERSATION puts all of these elements together into a natural interaction. There's no script for a real conversation, but one example might be something like this:

❖ Your friend mentions an *experience*.

❖ You *ask open-ended questions* to let your friend *tell the story* of his experience. Storytelling lets you hear how he understands his experience. You stick with questions until you're confident that you've heard his story.

❖ You *reflect* on what you heard. You engage with your friend about his experience based on what you heard. You might connect his experience to something about your shared humanity. You don't give advice or get preachy. You listen to his response without arguing. You use questions to invite him to say what he thinks. You share your experience without changing the focus to you.

❖ You *conclude* the conversation by pulling out a life principle from the discussion. You use the raw material of his experience so that he has genuinely become his own teacher. He should walk away from this conversation not feeling that he's been lectured to. (Not every conversation leads magically to a life principle. Don't be too focused on this goal. Avoid going into a conversation thinking, *I must get this conversation to a point where I can draw out a life principle!* Your goal is to care for the person, not drive him.)

❖ You act on what you learned from the conversation (if action is warranted).

7. What have you learned from this session that will make a real difference in your life as an insider?

GROUP EXERCISE

Let two participants practice holding a spiritual conversation about one participant's experience. The rest of the group will observe. After fifteen minutes, discuss what happened. (If the "Christian" in this scenario gets stuck, he or she can ask for coaching: What would be a good question at this point? How can I say *this* in nonreligious language? What could I possibly say about our common humanity?)

CASE STUDY

Imagine that, like Mike in the opening story, you're an elementary school teacher. You sit down in the teacher's lounge, and another teacher says, "How do they expect me to teach a class of thirty-five students with only twenty-nine books?" How do you proceed to have a conversation that is "full of grace, seasoned with salt"?

8. Some people feel they could never hold a spiritual conversation well. They forget the great questions. They lock up when they try to say something important in nonreligious language. They're so busy remembering the techniques that they forget simply to listen!

What counsel would you give someone who feels inadequate in this area?

GROUP EXERCISE

Share with your group one opportunity you had this week to converse the faith. It could be an opportunity you missed at the time. For example, the subject of possessions came up, but you didn't know what to say that wouldn't sound religious or preachy. Or you could have asked questions to go deeper with someone, but you didn't. Or you could have listened better. Brainstorm with your group about what you could have said.

"MY FRIENDS DON'T SEEM INTERESTED."

Exploring the Bible

*   *   *

Introducing the Bible into our relationships and then using it with unbelievers is a vital part of the insider's ministry. One of the most important things we can do for our friends is to motivate them to read the Bible. Conversing the faith will help because it will introduce the idea that we get insights about life from the Bible. However, there comes a point when we want to help our friends explore the Bible for themselves.

1. When you think about the unbelievers you know, what barriers would you need to overcome to see them interact with you over the Scriptures?

> ### *The* INSIDER
>
> Along with this session, read chapter 16 of *The Insider*.
>
> What questions does this reading raise?

INCARNATE RATHER THAN PROMOTE

JUST AS EVANGELISM is a process, introducing people to the Scriptures is also a process. Step 1 is "Incarnate rather than promote." People need to see us live out the reality of the Scriptures before they encounter the Scriptures themselves. They meet the Bible through the lives of people—us. We need boldness, and the appropriate language, to authentically share the interplay between our lifestyle, attitudes, values, and response to circumstances on the one hand, and what we are learning from the Bible on the other hand. As we do this, people see the Bible as relevant and having real value.

DEALING WITH INADEQUACY

If you feel you don't have the gifts to guide people through Scripture, don't despair. Nobody has all the gifts to be the perfect insider. That's why you'll discuss partnering in session 11. Maybe somebody in your group has the gifts to guide a discussion, while you are gifted to serve people, host a group, converse the faith, or pray.

---

2. What are some ways the Holy Spirit has used or is using the Bible in your life? Try to put this into nonreligious language.

PERSONAL EXERCISE

YOU DON'T NEED to be a Bible expert to incarnate the Scriptures. You just need to be learning something from the Bible on a regular basis. If the Bible plays no role in helping you figure out how to live your life, your friends aren't going to be drawn to it. If you need to start small, try taking time twice a week to read a chapter of the gospel of Matthew. As you read, ask yourself, "What does this have to do with my life, my values, my attitudes, and my response to my circumstances?"

When you read something that seems to connect with your life, write it down. Tell somebody (you can start with a Christian friend) what you saw. When you read something you don't understand, write it down. Find somebody you can ask about this.

Look for Evidence That They're Asking the Big Questions

AS WE PRAY and live authentically, we may find our friends beginning to ask questions about life and its meaning. Sometimes a crisis precipitates this shift. Slowly they begin to consider the possibility of a spiritual dimension to life. They wonder if perhaps God is real and relevant. Perhaps he can be known personally. This is fertile ground to plant the idea of reading the Scriptures. We should introduce the Bible as a resource that speaks to their questions and longings. When people are open to the possibility of a spiritual reality, there is an intensity as you explore the Scriptures together.

Many people have found it helpful not to ask for an immediate response when asking their friends to read the Bible. It is better first to sow the seed of the idea of reading the Bible together before asking for a commitment. People generally go through four stages when confronted with a new idea:

1. Rejection
2. Tolerance
3. Acceptance
4. Embrace

3. What might be evidence that your friends are open to or considering the possibility of spiritual reality?

4. What are some ways you could plant the idea of getting together to read the Bible—either with a group or personally?

GROUP EXERCISE

Go back to the names of unbelievers you listed on page 10. Where are you in the process of introducing the Bible to your friends? What are the next steps of faith for you in the process?

If your friends are still indifferent or antagonistic to spiritual reality, then you don't want to rush to the Bible. Praying, taking initiatives, and conversing the faith may be your task for some time. However, it's never too early to start paying attention to how the Bible fits in your life. You can mention the Bible occasionally when you hold spiritual conversations. You can pray for your friends to be prepared to ask life's big questions.

WHEN IT'S TIME, TAKE THE RISK!

5. What goes through your mind when you think about introducing the Bible into your relationships with unbelievers?

Using the Bible with unbelievers can seem overwhelming. It appears much simpler to invite our friends and family to a church meeting. The idea of reading the Bible confronts insiders with a variety of fears:

❖ I don't know the Bible well enough. I won't know the answers to questions.

❖ How will I make sure it's not boring?

❖ Can I do this and still maintain our friendship?

On pages 89-94 are some principles for using the Bible with unbelievers. Read these principles with the following questions in mind.

6. Which of the ideas for using the Bible with unbelievers do you find especially helpful or thought-provoking? What ideas might work for your friends?

7. What questions do you have about any of the ideas?

8. Write down the names of any of your friends or associates who you think are ready to begin considering reading the Bible with you.

THE TURNING POINT: CONVERSION

As our friends engage in the Bible, some will accept Christ and surrender to him. Now they are discovering God and how to follow his way, but it continues to be a journey. People need one or more companions on this journey.

In this companionship, two pivotal points are right before and right after conversion. At both points, we need to remain a companion. At either point, it's especially easy to switch roles and become a teacher. However, this switch changes the relational dynamics and confuses our friends. We need to continue in a spirit of mutuality—both learners. Even if we have read the Bible for twenty years, we have not read it with these friends. We can learn much from them.

MIXED BIBLE-READING GROUPS

THE MIXED BIBLE-READING group is a small group of friends who meet together to read the Bible and reflect on its message and relevance to their lives.

It is called "mixed" because people are at different places in their spiritual journeys. All are learners, but not all are Christians.

It is deliberately referred to as a reading group, not a study group. The word *study*, when linked to the Bible, suggests precision, rationality, facts, definition, and cognitive activity to a generation more comfortable with ambiguity, intuition, and flexibility.

It is a group. To read the Bible alone has become more and more difficult for people. For an increasing number of people it is more motivating to read in a group. Reading the Bible with just one other individual can arouse a fear of being manipulated.

People value community. In our frantic consumer-oriented society, it is increasingly rare for people to experience meaningful community. Yet this is an essential component of our humanity. The mixed Bible-reading group provides a meeting place for community to emerge. Friendships deepen and people feel an increasing freedom to share personal and specific needs.

The mixed Bible-reading group can fulfill the following purposes:

- ❖ A simple forum that enables people to introduce their friends to the Scriptures. It has the potential to be generational; as people come to faith in Christ, they may want to invite their unbelieving friends to join.
- ❖ A safe place for continued growth as a follower of Jesus Christ—the creation of a spiritual home. It is a place where people can bring their life contexts and, through interaction with others and the Scriptures, move forward in their spiritual journeys.

PRINCIPLES FOR LEADING A BIBLE-READING GROUP

Leadership is essential, but not leadership in the traditional sense. It appears low-key and casual, but is actually very intentional.

1. *Be clear on what two things need to happen.*

   Understanding. People need to understand the gospel: who Jesus Christ is, why he did what he did, and what he wants of us in response. However, ignorance is not the real obstacle to faith.

   Submission. The real problem is rebellion. Sin is "everyone turning to his own way." Conversion is ending the rebellion; it is coming out with your hands up. Getting someone to agree that the resurrection has to be true or getting him to pray a prayer does not necessarily mean he is yielding his life to Christ's leadership.

2. *Understand the division of labor in evangelism.*

   The Scriptures speak the truth. They cut away the blindness and reveal our thoughts and attitudes (see Hebrews 4:12). This happens whether or not a person believes the Bible.

   The Holy Spirit convicts a person. He convicts of sin, of righteousness, and of judgment. He gives life (see John 16:4-11).

   We "show and tell." We love people and help them understand what is written in the Scriptures (see 1 John 1:2-3). We tend to overstep this role and try to do the work of the Holy Spirit and the Scriptures. This leaves us attempting to do the impossible and frustrates both us and those to whom we minister. *It is not our job to press people to understand the gospel or submit to Christ.* Our job is to provide a safe place in which people can discover Christ and find out what following him would involve.

3. *There is no need to prove the authority of the Scriptures.*

   We have observed that the Bible begins to have increasing authority in the group. It speaks for itself.

4. Plan the logistics of the group carefully.

- *Fun and atmosphere help.* The ambience of where we meet contributes to the evening. We try to stay with casual meeting places (a home, a coffee house). Occasionally we will do something special. Initially some people come for this reason alone!
- *Regularity helps.* We meet biweekly. Any more often than this is unattainable. Any less lacks continuity.
- *Size matters.* About six couples seem to be the maximum number. It allows for participation but also means that when some people are absent, the group can continue to meet.
- *Affinity helps.* A common shared life context allows for greater group ownership of the discussion. It also facilitates social interaction.

5. Ownership belongs to the group.

The group does not belong to anyone other than those in the group—not just the leader, not just the Christians in the group, and not a church. We do not want people to miss the opportunity to read the Bible because they think to do so also involves commitment to some organization beyond the group. Likewise, the Bible-reading group is not a door to something more formal. It is not an outpost of a larger context to which we try to recruit.

6. Go into the discussion as a learner among learners.

There is always more to learn about Christ and becoming like him. Realize that you are on the same journey as the unbeliever. He or she needs to submit to Christ and follow him. So do you. The goal for both is found in Ephesians 4:13.

This is difficult for some of us. We know we're learners, but we've learned some things already, and we want others to learn those things too. We must get ourselves to the point at which we genuinely believe that this will be a personal journey of discovery we have not taken before.

We must also remind ourselves that even an unbeliever has something valuable to offer from his interaction with the Scriptures and his particular life context. We will learn something new about God and ourselves if we listen.

7. *Be prepared for the discussion — but don't let it show.*

- Pray!

- Understand the Bible passage you are going to discuss. Meditate on it. Let it speak to you first.

- Prepare a few questions that will direct people into the big ideas of the passage.

- Be prepared to simply and succinctly explain the critical ideas of the chapter. Use these explanations only if necessary. At all costs, avoid becoming the teacher.

8. *Give people the space they need to think.*

They need room to doubt, wrestle with the truths they encounter, and weigh the cost of their decisions to submit to Christ. We need to create an environment that encourages thinking. This takes skill. Space to think is difficult to create and easily destroyed. It is destroyed when we as facilitators:

- Talk more than listen.

- Give answers more than ask questions.

- Use chapter and verse to prove that we are right and the others are wrong. (Cross-references should be used to bring additional information into the discussion, not as proof texts.)

Remember that the real issue in evangelism is the submission of the will to Christ. The temptation to try to win every point in the discussion can actually work against that happening. Our need to win can generate resistance — against us, and consequently, against the gospel!

9. *Be more interested in getting people to express their own thoughts than in expressing yours.*

This means:

- Being an active, attentive listener.
- Welcoming questions, not being threatened by them.
- Probing a participant's comments with additional questions when you suspect "there is more where that came from."

Establish an atmosphere of freedom. Let people know they're free to share their doubts, encouragements, struggles, joys, and insights, as well as their thoughts on the Scriptures. The response of others in the group will facilitate or hinder this. The willingness of people to share freely is vital.

10. *Enable full participation.*

All members of the group need to be able to contribute. It is too easy for a few articulate participants to dominate the conversation. Some Christians feel compelled to have an answer or move to fix a life situation shared in the group. This is death to a reading group.

Methods to aid full participation include:

- *Encouraging.* "Who else wants to say something?" or "Could we hear from someone who hasn't talked for a while?"
- *Balancing.* This is useful when most members appear reticent to disagree with someone in the group. "Does everyone see it that way, or are there other points of view?" or "What are some other ways of looking at this?" are questions that can lend support to people who do not agree with the predominant point of view.
- *Making space.* This involves questions or supportive statements focused on specific individuals. "Frank, you look like you want to say something—do you?" or "We only have time for one or two more comments; perhaps we could hear from someone who hasn't spoken for a while."

- *Using the clock.* "We have five minutes left. I want to make sure we've heard from everyone who wants to speak, particularly those who haven't had a chance yet." Or, "We only have time for one or two more comments. Perhaps we could hear from someone who hasn't spoken for a while."

11. *Paint a picture that enables the group to step into the text.*

There are times when it's helpful to stimulate the group's imagination by fleshing out the text through storytelling. The more we are able to help people step into the original context, the more they'll be able to connect with the text at a heart level. To do this, you'll need to do some background reading on the original context. A Bible dictionary can provide this. Again, avoid lecturing the group with every tidbit you glean from your research. Less is more. ("Here's Jesus in Samaria, where a Jew would have . . ." "It's the hottest part of the day . . .")

12. *Build a bridge through questions.*

Ask open-ended questions that promote the interaction of heart, mind, biblical text, and one's life. Your primary questions might aim to help participants understand what the text means. But you should also—sparingly—ask questions that help people connect what they're reading to their life experience. For example, "Is there anything we're reading today that speaks into a situation you're currently facing?" Avoid putting people on the spot (it might be best not to lean on people to personally apply passages about sin), but do help them make life connections (with a passage that offers a strategy for dealing with suffering or relationships, for instance).

> ### HELPFUL LAUNCHING QUESTIONS
>
> - As we read the passage, did any part of it stir you?
> - What did you feel as we read the passage?
> - What situations, circumstances, and memories from your own life came to mind as you listened?
> - What from the passage would you love to be true of you?
> - What from the passage surprised, angered, or puzzled you?
> - What do you think the original recipients heard when they encountered this passage?
> - What does it say to your situation?
> - What do you think is important in this passage? Why is it important? In what ways is it important to you?

13. *Keep the discussion on track.*

A rambling discussion meets no one's needs and frustrates everyone. Your job is to consistently bring the discussion back to the biblical text. Keep in mind that you're together to help each other understand what is written in the Scriptures.

14. *Don't be afraid of silence. People need time to think.*

15. *Watch your timing, your pace.*

Be sensitive to how long you should spend on each subject. Go for the big ideas of the passage. Resist the urge to dig into all the details that are there. Know when to move on. Quit before the group does.

16. *Occasionally summarize the truths you have covered.*

Sometimes a summary is a good occasion to give a succinct explanation of the gospel. This helps clarify the fact that this message calls for a response. Most spiritual births take place without a third party precipitating the decision. Nevertheless, sometimes it becomes obvious that the understanding and the desire are there, but the person needs our help in taking the step.

However, don't feel compelled to summarize every discussion. Welcome open discussion and resist having to bring closure. Truth will emerge when the Scriptures are in play.

17. *Maintain a sense of progress.*

If you ever want to get rid of someone, just take a month to plod through one chapter of the Bible with him. Try to get through a chapter at every meeting.

18. *Remember that at the beginning your friend is committed to you for only one session at a time.*

Even in later stages only you will be aware of the extensiveness of the process.

RESOURCES

"Twenty-Four Hours with John" is a Bible study written with unbelievers in mind. The full text is available in the book *Living Proof* by Jim Petersen (NavPress, 1989). "Twenty-Four Hours with John" is particularly suitable for those unbelievers interested in examining the life of Christ. The questions are focused, and the leader sets the direction and asks the questions.

Other resources include:

- *Straight to the Source* video, 1800 McCollie Ave., Chattanooga, TN 37404, 800-566-2262, www.cbmc.com

- *The Message — The Bible in Contemporary Language* by Eugene Peterson (NavPress, 2002).

- *The Bible Overview* by Larry Ebert, available from Chuck Strittmater, on Navigator staff in Des Moines, Iowa or from The Bible Overview, 2060 Stonington Avenue, Suite 202, Hoffman Estates, IL 60195.

- *Living Like a Missionary* (Creation Resources version 3.1, 2000)

- *Thinking Like a Missionary* (Creation Resources version 3.1, 2000)

"I CAN'T DO THIS ALONE."

Partnering with Others

✳   ✳   ✳

By now you are realizing there is no way you can go it alone as an insider. By yourself you don't have what it takes. Yet the habits of individualism run deep. It's not easy to change, but if you don't, you will remain limited as an insider.

You've seen that a small group of believers and unbelievers meeting together to discuss the Bible is an important part of the insider's ministry. However, this requires time and effort to be sustainable.

1. What functions have to be fulfilled for a discussion group to work? *examples: planning, hospitality.*

   Which of these can be fulfilled only by believers?

> ### *The* INSIDER
>
> Along with this session, read chapter 15 of *The Insider*.
>
> What questions does this reading raise?

2. What are some other functions of insidership that need to go on at the same time? *examples: Hospitality toward those not yet ready to join the group, little initiatives, praying for the Holy Spirit to act in people's lives.*

   Which of these are strengths for you?

GROUP EXERCISE

By completing this workbook, you've accomplished something significant. Plan an opportunity to celebrate after session 12. For example, share a meal together. Begin the meal by giving each person an opportunity to say what he or she is grateful for regarding the group. For what would you like to thank your group? Then spend the rest of your time just enjoying each other.

If you want to end your group on a really high point, ask all participants to think ahead of time about the specific strengths they see in each group member. When you meet, take each person in turn. The rest of the group points out gifts and strengths they see in that person that he or she has to offer as an insider. Then you move to the next person. This will take about forty-five minutes, but people will probably remember what you say about them for the rest of their lives. We rarely get a chance to hear the positive things that others see in us.

In which areas could you use some help?

3. Where are you currently on the scale of practicing interdependence?

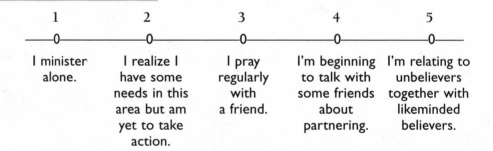

1	2	3	4	5
I minister alone.	I realize I have some needs in this area but am yet to take action.	I pray regularly with a friend.	I'm beginning to talk with some friends about partnering.	I'm relating to unbelievers together with likeminded believers.

4. When it comes to partnering with others as insiders, what challenges do you face?

Trust Builders	Trust Destroyers
Openness. Let's consider and explore our issues.	*Hiddenness.* I can resolve issues on my own. I do not see or admit the problem.
Affirmation. That's a great point.	*Criticism.* How can you think something like that?
Submission. I come under your influence too.	
Clear communication of truth. Let's see what the Bible says.	*Competition.* My influence is better than yours.
Protection. I can learn and grow.	*Avoidance of truth.* I don't know what you're talking about. I don't do that.
Appropriate initiatives. I properly and graciously bring up options to meet needs.	*Blame.* It has to be somebody's fault.
Thankfulness. It is good to have others like you partnering with me in this.	*Perfection* is the standard.
	Ingratitude. I can't believe I have to put up with all this.
Serving. I hope to give of myself in a properly balanced way.	*Me first.* Let me tell you what I have going on before you finish that thought.
Listening/Apologizing. Have I confused/offended you? I'm sorry.	*Excuses.* There is a good reason for this—let me explain (defensiveness).
Grace. You are free to be imperfect.	*Legalism.* I judge and control.
Integrity. I admit the truth about who I really am.	*Image protection.* I manipulate your view of me.
Humility. I may be wrong and have lots to learn.	*I am right.* There is a wrong way and my way.
Clear expectations.	*Unspoken and differing expectations.* I assumed you knew I never wanted to be spoken to that way.

5. Read the lists of trust builders and trust destroyers. Which qualities are especially important to you in relationships?

THE IMPORTANCE OF TRUST

Trust is vital to partnering. Trust frees people to contribute.

In which of these character qualities do you most need to grow?

In discussing community, the Scriptures emphasize function rather than form. In fact, the Scriptures have hardly anything to say about form. Rather, community is the living out of the "one-anothers."

Function is what needs to be accomplished (such as encouraging one another). *Form* is the pattern or method of fulfilling the function (such as a weekly breakfast meeting). Both are needed. Functions are expressed within appropriate forms. However, too often we assume that if we have the form, we have the function. We make the two synonymous. If we are congregating, we can assume we have love and trust and partnership in the gospel. Confusing the two robs the insider of the freedom to use a variety of forms to meaningfully express interdependence.

6. What are some forms that would enable you to express biblical interdependence in ways that keep you involved with unbelievers? *example: Function — encourage one another daily (see Hebrews 10:24-25). Form — phone my insider partner to discuss how my encounters with unbelievers at work went this week.*

7. Who in your circle of Christian friends shares your desire to live as an insider?

8. Who can be naturally involved with you and your unbelieving friends?

9. Who has gifts and strengths that would complement you in areas in which you're less strong?

10. Who can help or coach you in living as an insider?

11. What specific steps can you take to partner in living as an insider?

GROUP EXERCISE

In what ways have you already been partnering with the others in your group?

In what ways would you be interested in partnering with the others in this group after you complete this workbook? (Be honest with one another about your desires. Some in the group may be eager to move forward, while others may be struggling with busyness or other obstacles. Where are you—truly—on the road to being an insider?)

What would you need from partners?

What do you have to offer a partnership?

"WHERE TO FROM HERE?"

Midwifing the New Birth

✳   ✳   ✳

Conversion demands a choice to end one's rebellion against God. If we want him in our lives, we must be willing to end the war, to come out with our hands up. This is hard on one's ego and that's why it's difficult. That's also why it can take months, often years, for a person to decide to take this vital step. We need to be patient.

Our popular notion of conversion is very different from this. Our focus tends to be on the *act* of making the decision rather than on the submission of the heart to Christ. Many churches and mission organizations orient their programs around calling people to visibly perform the act. As a result, over the past several decades, thousands of conversions have been recorded in country after country all over the world, but often with minimal enduring results.

1. Read chapter 17 of *The Insider.* What's your response to the way conversion is defined there? If it differs from your previous understanding of conversion, what are the differences?

The INSIDER

Along with this session, read chapter 17 of *The Insider.* If possible also read chapters 18 and 19.

What questions does this reading raise?

GROUP EXERCISE

This session is your last official group meeting. Think about how members of your group might pursue a long-range plan together.

2. Think back to the time when you came to faith in Christ. To what extent did you understand that real faith involved a commitment to start living the way Jesus taught under the power of the Holy Spirit? How did your understanding affect your spiritual growth?

PASSING ON THE VISION

Conversion is the beginning of a new and radically different life . . . We take on a new identity. The new way of life we are stepping into is brimming with purpose. Peter goes on to explain that God's intention is that we "declare the praises of him who called [us] out of darkness into his wonderful light." And he says that this happens as we live "such good lives among the pagans that . . . they may see [our] good deeds and glorify God."[9] We are called to live, today, as the citizens of his eternal kingdom that we are.

New believers need to catch this vision of what they have become—and of what they are becoming. And they need help in getting from where they are to where God intends for them to be. This will inevitably require some early healing—and then a lifetime of growing.

—THE INSIDER, PAGE 201

---

3. Again, think about your own faith decision. How much help did you have at that time from mature Christians in figuring out how to go about following Christ? How did that experience affect your spiritual growth?

4. If one of your unbelieving friends lets you know that he or she had come to believe that Jesus was the Son of God and was raised from the dead, what would be your next move?

Next Steps

TAKE TIME TO review and pray over your notes from this workbook.

5. Look at the names you listed on page 10. In what ways have these people benefited from the time you have spent using this workbook?

6. What major lessons have you learned? What insights have you gained?

7. What insights and lessons are you excited about?

8. What things are crucial for you to change?

9. What adjustments are you making in the way you live?

10. What challenges do you still need to overcome?

11. What steps can you take to deal with these challenges?

12. When you think about the next year of your life, how do you see your insidership unfolding?

Notes

*　*　*

1. Rodney Stark, *The Rise of Christianity* (San Francisco, Calif.: HarperCollins, 1997), p. 208.

2. Stark, p. 208.

3. See *The Insider,* p. 58.

4. Based on an unpublished article by Don Bartel.

5. Richard Swenson, *The Overload Syndrome: Learning to Live Within Your Limits* (Colorado Springs, Colo.: NavPress, 1998), p. 44.

6. See *The Insider,* p. 169.

7. See *The Insider,* p. 169.

8. Jerry D. Jones, *201 Great Questions* (Colorado Springs, Colo.: NavPress, 1999).

9. 1 Peter 2:9,12.

AUTHORS

*   *   *

MIKE SHAMY has led the The Navigators' mission to U.S. metro areas since 1999. Through his ministry in New Zealand, Australia, and the United Kingdom, Mike has gained practical experience of what is needed to be an insider in increasingly post-Christian cultures. He and his wife, Audrey, now live in Colorado Springs, Colorado, where they seek to personally live as insiders as well as help others to do the same. They are the parents of four adult children.

JIM PETERSEN is the associate to the general director of The Navigators. He helped pioneer the Navigator ministry in Brazil, developed missionary teams in Latin America, and coached ministry teams around the world. Through living and ministering in many nations and cultures, Jim has acquired practical experience in applying biblical principles to life and ministry. He shares this in his books *Living Proof, Church Without Walls,* and *Lifestyle Discipleship* (all NavPress). Jim and his wife, Marge, have raised four children and live in Colorado Springs.

MORE THOUGHT-PROVOKING TITLES BY JIM PETERSEN.

The Insider

Evangelism is not just for the gifted few—it's for all of us. This paradigm-changing book will give you the awareness and skills you need to share your faith with the people in your everyday relational circles.

By Jim Petersen and Mike Shamy

Living Proof

Evangelism is more than just a sweaty-palmed speech to a stranger on the street. It should begin with a lifestyle that is Living Proof.

By Jim Petersen

Lifestyle Discipleship

"Behavior begins with values, and values stem from a person's worldview. Until discipleship speaks to people at that level, there will be very little spiritual growth to speak of." (excerpt from the book)

By Jim Petersen

To order copies, visit your local Christian bookstore, call NavPress at 1-800-366-7788, or log on to www.navpress.com.

To locate a Christian bookstore near you, call 1-800-991-7747.

NAVPRESS
BRINGING TRUTH TO LIFE
www.navpress.com